PlayType

PlayTypes

Speculations and Possibilities

by

Bob Hughes

Edited by

Gordon Sturrock

Commissioned by The London Centre for Playwork Education and Training

Researched and written by Bob Hughes
For further information please contact played@dial.pipex.com or visit: www.playeducation.com

Edited by Gordon Sturrock

ISBN 10   0-9554320-0-6
ISBN 13   978-0-9554320-0-2

Published and Distributed by
The London Centre for Playwork Education and Training
Block D, Barnsbury Complex
Offord Road
London N1 1QG
ncpelondon@aol.com

Design, typesetting and production by
Action Publishing Techhology Ltd, Gloucester
Printed in Great Britain

One dog barks a warning. The others bark at him.

Chinese Proverb

Dedicated to Tom, Finnian and Elijah, and to the memory of Frank King.

Contents

Acknowledgements

Writing this book has been a demanding emotional and intellectual exercise for me, and I am very grateful for the help, support and encouragement I have received from numerous sources during the production of the manuscript.

In particular I want to thank Bridget Handscomb and John Fitzpatrick for their hard work and patience in bringing this publication to fruition. I am also deeply grateful to Janine Brady for her valuable advice, searching questions and encouragement.

I also thank The London Centre for Playwork Education and Training for commissioning and publishing this work.

My sincere thanks also go to my friend and colleague Gordon Sturrock for editing the manuscript and for invaluable advice and rigour.

I must acknowledge the contribution made by my part-time employment at Islington Play Association. At times this has been a difficult journey and I worried whether any useful purpose could be served in writing a book such as this. It was the regular visits to Islington's playgrounds and the observations I made of children playing during those visits, made possible by that employment, that rescued me from those fears.

I should also express my gratitude to the authors and editors of all the publications whose work has been an inspiration. Especially,

Marc Bekoff, John A. Byers and all the contributing authors for *Animal Play*.

Gordon M. Burghardt for *The Genesis of Animal Play*.

Anthony Stevens and John Price for *Evolutionary Psychiatry*.

Brian Sutton-Smith for *The Ambiguity of Play*.

Finally, I thank all of my family for their forbearance when I went into 'writing mode', especially my partner Annie for her endless patience.

Foreword

It gives all of us at the LCPET great pleasure to have supported the development of this work from its inception as an initial idea through to its fruition as our first book as publishers.

Since LCPET was established in 1991 we have been committed to ensuring that the field has access to good quality materials and resources which support and develop our shared knowledge and understanding of play and playwork. We have combined access to materials with professional development opportunites to enhance the standard of education and training offered in the sector.

Two years ago we identified the need to increase opportunities to understand the theory of playtypes. It is integral to the theoretical knowledge-base of quality assurance, the National Occupational Standards in Playwork and the playwork education and training curriculum. We recognised that there was a gap in existing materials and resources and a need to gain a deeper understanding of the theory and how to apply it within the sector.

We were delighted when Bob Hughes accepted our invitation to write more on the subject. Much has occured since then and we have all benefited from the subsequent partnership that has developed. It has been a pleasure to work with Bob, who has been highly committed, challenging and productive in this enterprise.

Our intention was to help further a shared understanding on this subject without over-simplifying or narrowing down this emergent theory. Many questions will have further light shed on them but in many ways this book will probably leave you with even more questions than before as it explores new areas of an even more complex nature. What we do hope is that it helps to continue to stimulate and increase your interest and motivation to learn and to promote the importance of play.

London Centre for Playwork Education and Training

September 2006

Introduction

Prior to 1996 it is doubtful whether many of those in playwork, early years or childcare had even heard of playtypes, let alone thought much about them. Yet, as I write, ten years later, they have become an integral part of playwork's 'Industry Standard' and, as a consequence, something that new playworkers have to know about and all other playworkers need to be familiar with and be able to use as a tool to explore and assess their practice.

But what on earth are playtypes? What are they for? Where have they come from and why have they struck such a chord within playwork and other child-related professions?

Perhaps even more importantly: why should anyone, playworkers or others who work with children, care about this theoretical tool? The question that arises is: what is the point of expending time and energy making something that every child does anyway appear so deep and complicated?

In the following pages I attempt to address these questions and others, to provide some thought-provoking theorising about the evolution of playtypes and their importance to human survival and sanity.

'Playtypes' is the term we use to describe the different visible behaviours we observe when children are playing. The reasons we are interested in them are two-fold. Firstly, if we assume that manifesting each one is beneficial in some way to the child, then it falls to those who provide environments, props and resources for play to ensure that each playtype is enabled and catered for.

However, it is the second reason for our interest that is the main focus for this book. It is my conviction, and this is increasingly supported by the literature, that whether children manifest each playtype, and how those playtypes are manifested is, in some way not yet fully understood, an indication of deeper processes taking place within the organism that we call the child.

These processes may provide clues to the child's day-to-day health and well-being, but more importantly, they may manifest symptoms of an evolutionary unease which is being experienced, if that is the right word, by the organism and channelled through its most powerful and comprehensive form of communication, its play.

Play may not only be the evolutionary mechanism whereby the child adapts, it may also act as the evolutionary detector, which tells the child that it has to. Whether it then can, or not, whether it can playfully escape the ever present pressures of extinction that are the other side of the adaptive coin, may be reflected in the content of its playtypes as manifested in its play. If it is not adapting, or for whatever reason, is not able to, it may well show its distress at not adapting, in the way it plays.

This book attempts to answer the questions inherent in the statements above. What it does, is begin a survey of the playtypes landscape and undertake a tentative reconnoitre of what might lie beyond what we already know, using recent empirical and other theoretical material as its only available landmarks. It does so from the perspective of a novel new idea I have called neuroludic-evolutionary theory.

When I use the term *neuroludic-evolutionary theory*, what I am suggesting is that play is a more formative product of, and influence on, the evolutionary process than is generally recognised; that there is an evolutionary predisposition of elements of brain activity and neural growth that are dependent not only upon children playing, but upon children engaging equally in each playtype. And that if children do not experience play comprehensively and as evolution has predisposed, then not only will this brain activity and neural growth not happen, but the resultant deprivation will act to psychically destabilise the affected child, with catastrophic results.

Whether what has been deduced by the end of the book has increased our understanding of the playtypes phenomena, is for you the reader, to decide. For myself, it is my belief that as a species, we are only just beginning an important journey into the relationship between play and the evolutionary forces that created it, a journey that may also incorporate a race for our species survival.

The text of *PlayTypes – Speculations and Possibilities* has been divided into three parts that reflect the book's gradual move from known practice to deep theory.

Part I. Chapters One to Four look in detail at the playtypes as they appear in the original Taxonomy of PlayTypes. Chapter One is in fact an abridged version of a paper I gave in 2005. It provides a brief overview of the processes that led to this book.

Chapter Two explores some of the historical context to the development of the Taxonomy and my quest to better understand playtypes. Chapter Three provides a more in-depth exploration of what different playtypes are and how we might better recognise them. Chapter Four analyses playtypes in the context of four of playwork's main considerations – the increasing **complexity** of our understanding of play; the need for **comprehensiveness** in the experiences playwork offers children; the recognition that the play environment must offer **compensation** for play experience deficits in the built environment; and the increasing role of the play environment in counteracting the effects of play **deprivation** in the modern world.

Part II. Chapter Five, Types of PlayTypes, explores the factors that may affect how we perceive playtypes. It focuses on the notion of 'spectra', and reflects on how a child's ontology, play intensity and psychic state may affect how their playtypes are manifested. Chapter Six explores whether simple playtypes amalgamate or merge into more complex forms.

Part III. Chapter Seven explores ideas stimulated by MacLean's

Triune Brain Theory. Are the playtypes we observe generated in three quite different neural structures? If they are, could there be three distinct versions of each playtype, or does each playtype reflect the reptilian, emotional and rational components of the Triune Brain? Are playtypes mutations from, or isotopes of, their originals?

I hope you will find it useful food for thought.

Bob Hughes
Ely
June 2006

PART I

Chapter One

Introduction

Chapter One is drawn from a paper the author gave at the London Centre for Playwork Education and Training's Conference in London in June 2005. As it flags up some of the new ideas that are outlined later it acts both as an introduction to the chapters that follow and the thinking they contain.

Of particular relevance is the review of some of the findings in the more recent literature regarding play and playtypes and their role in the process of human evolution. However, it is the discussions relating to the structure and evolution of the human brain and its implications for the number and possible function of different playtypes that the reader may find most interesting

More About PlayTypes – Reflections and Developments

When I originally accepted the invitation from the London Centre to write a follow-up to *A Playworker's Taxonomy of PlayTypes*, I did not foresee any particular problem with the idea. I would need to do a literature search on developments relating to playtypes since 1996, the year the Taxonomy was written, report back on them, feed in my own thoughts and that would probably be that.

But life is rarely that simple. And, in a field as complex, multi-layered and fast evolving as playwork, I should have known better.

This field has become much more technical since the time when Sandra Melville, the then Director of PLAYLINK, with whom I was working at the time, initially suggested I write a taxonomy of play-types. Playtypes have become an integral part of the language of playwork and of playworkers. They have also become a part of the so-described Industry Standard and, as such, are judged as something all playworkers need to know about.

Now, nearly a decade on, I find myself reflecting on what has happened in the meantime, in terms of my understanding of the idea of playtypes.

No one was more surprised than I, when the Taxonomy gained in popularity and playtypes began to become a part of playworkers' everyday professional mindset. In 2002, I revised and tried to improve the Taxonomy and did not think much more about it.

Then along came the invitation to write an update. I did my literature search and, as I suspected, not much had changed. I wondered if there was a need for a new publication at all.

Then, as often happens when we are thinking and reading prior to writing, a creative process began, over which I had little control. Questions and ideas came into my consciousness from every area of my thought processes and suddenly it seemed that things had moved forward significantly.

As a result, what I would like to do now is to reflect on this re-visitation and where it has taken me. Some of it is fairly off the wall, but then its impact on my imagination has always been a reliable indicator of how fertile a particular area is, and I have faithfully followed these considerations. Typical of the way that I work this has resulted in the creation of a new theoretical construct based on an idea that I am describing as neuroludic-evolutionary theory. What follows is my first essay into exploring this radical new idea.

The literature

Since writing the original Taxonomy I have read and written a lot of material and, as a consequence, I now have many questions about playtypes that need much deeper analysis than I can do justice to here. However, I feel it important to at least set out the context for this further thinking.

One book, entitled *Animal Play*, has made a particularly significant contribution to this process and a huge impression on me. Edited by Marc Bekoff and John Byers, it was published by Cambridge University Press in 1998 and is one of the few books on play, of weight, for at least a decade. The impact of this book on my view of playtypes has been extraordinary. In particular, it has made it possible for me to pull away from playtypes as my horizon and to see them in a more evolutionary context.

Animal Play is full of vital information about the importance of playtypes to our survival, our evolution and to our physiological and psychological development. For example Burghardt (1998) writes that

> one of the problems of defining, studying and interpreting play is that it is most certainly a heterogeneous category. (p. 6)

He suggests that different play 'types' may have different causal bases, functions, phylogenies and ontogenies. That is, play has a number of subdivisions, which have each appeared for different reasons, do different things, and have come into existence at different periods in evolutionary time.

As Burghardt is suggesting, if some playtypes are younger from an evolutionary perspective than some others, it follows that children from earlier human evolutionary stages may have drawn from a repertoire that contained fewer playtypes than does our current evolutionary stage. If that is the case, we can deduce, for example, that different playtypes will have evolved at different times during our evolution and that children in the future will evolve new playtypes currently unknown to us. The process is probably happening as I speak.

Reflecting on this, I found myself asking: what first triggered the evolution of playtypes, which playtype was the first, and why was it a particular playtype and not another one? I found myself stumbling into areas such as cellular energy transfer, autopoiesis and Mitchell's Chemiosmotic Theory, whilst trying to determine: Does playtypes development come from an 'intelligent' internal source? What is it that drives the evolution of playtypes? Where does its energy come from? How do we all end up with the same playtypes?

Was it even possible, as it has been with the Periodic Table of the Elements, for example, to forecast, *which* playtypes might evolve in the future and whether any had been lost to us in the past? Could future playtypes be identified by studying the nature and evolutionary order of playtypes already in existence? And, because of the long-established relationship between playtypes and adaptation, could we learn to forecast the adaptive trends or events, which in the past may have caused playtypes to evolve in the first place? This would be a hugely important development, because we would then be able to forecast future threats to our existence as organisms, using these emerging playtypes.

In another passage, Burghardt, ibid., states

These authors presented evidence suggesting that play behaviour in some juvenile mammals may permanently modify muscle fibre differentiation and cerebellar synapse distribution ... the changes posited ... are permanent and unlikely to be induced by other behavioural means. (p. 18)

Previously, the link with brain growth established by Rozenzweig *et al.* in 1962 had been environmental, but this confirmed what Sutton-Smith (1997) had reported; that there is a direct connection between playing and muscle and brain development. We can infer from this that when children play their brain and muscles are altered as a result of the experience and that these changes are permanent.

This link between play and what is known as brain plasticity is made even clearer later, when Byers (1998) writes of house mice, Norway rats and domestic cats:

> in these three species, play is turned on when there is an opportunity for experience-dependent modification of the cerebellum, and it is turned off shortly after the architecture of the cerebellum is complete. (p. 214)

This confirms that play and brain plasticity are not just linked, but that one of the reasons play evolved was actually to enhance the growth and structure of the brain. Reflecting on this, I found myself wondering: If play enhances brain growth, do different playtypes enhance the growth of different parts of the brain?

The appearance of playtypes in individuals always occurs during a specific time frame. Known in biology as a 'sensitive period' it is defined by Byers (ibid.) as

> a window in development during which specific types of experience (in this case, play) permanently alter the course of the development of the brain ... [a] development which is not possible before or after the window. (p. 210)

In children this window seems to occur between birth and about eight years of age.

The sensitive period is thought to be so influential in children that it caused the neurologist Huttenlocher (1990, 1992), cited in Sutton-Smith (1997), to conclude from brain imaging data he had collected, that children under ten years of age had twice the potential brain capacity of children over ten. This would mean that if children aged between 0 and 8 – the sensitive period – engaged in the full range of playtypes they would have their brain size, neurochemical activity, neural capacity and processing capability greatly enhanced; the converse of this being that these benefits would be adversely affected if children did not experience regular exposure to each playtype during the first eight years of their lives.

To recap: I propose that phenomena we call playtypes:

- originate from what I perceive as an 'intelligent internal source' and by that I mean a source which is genetically programmed to generate the same specific playtypes in every child in our species;
- originate during the same ontological period – childhood;
- originate for the same biological purposes in each child;
- have a prominent role in brain and muscle development;
- may affect the same discrete areas of brain development;
- occur during a biologically sensitive period of 0–8 years;
- may be increasing in number over evolutionary time;
- may be able to be used to predict future adaptive needs.

In practical terms this means that we should ensure that all children have regular access to each of the playtypes, from at least birth to 8 years of age. All this poses a new reality on playwork's interpretation of development, particularly, as I will go on to say, in the area of brain plasticity and synaptic activity.

The triune brain

Another avenue of my reflection has been informed by the field of Evolutionary Psychiatry, in particular the relationship between playtypes and the work of the neuroscientist Paul MacLean. In 1976, MacLean proposed that the human brain is really three brains in one; three brains that can communicate but, in his words,

> each with a different phylogenetic history, each with its own special intelligence, its own special memory, its own sense of time and space, and its own motor functions. (p. 180)

Or, as he states in a later paper (1985),

> Radically different in their chemistry and structure and in an evolutionary sense, aeons apart. (p. 219)

These structures he called the 'triune brain'.

What he proposed was that the brain evolved in three stages and that each of these stages was retained and became an intrinsic part of the total human brain we know today. This is similar to the notion of human beings being compounds (Wilber), or recapitulations (Hall), of all of their previous physical and or psychic/psychological evolutionary stages.

The core of the triune brain, the reptilian complex, MacLean said was responsible for instinctive reactions to events. The next layer he labelled the paleomammalian or limbic area. This consisted primarily of the limbic system, which was responsible for emotional reactions. The outer layer, and the most recent development in evolutionary terms, he called the neomammalian, or neocortex. This, he said, was responsible for rational thought.

What MacLean proposed was that each of these layers was autonomous, with its own life but that, although separate in many senses, each could communicate with the other. So our reaction to events could be the result of a combination of the interaction of all three, or of each one individually, or a combination of any two.

One is drawn to the idea of human actions and activity being created and governed by simultaneously competing and cooperating reptilian, primate and human currents.

Triune brain and play

However, what is the relevance of this to playtypes?

There are numerous implications. For example, might the genesis of different playtypes be located in specific sections of this triune brain, i.e. the reptilian section, the limbic section or the neocortex section? Alternatively, might each playtype have three different versions or components?

Although these specific questions will be explored in detail later, the immediate relevance of the triune model to playwork can be seen from the following *paraphrased* perspective from Stevens and Price (2000).

When a child enters a [play space] she brings with her, in a manner of speaking, a crowd of people from her past. That [play-work] has always known. What [evolutionary playwork] has recognised is that she also brings the hunter-gatherer, the primate and the reptile from her ancestral past too. The [play space] is crowded with this menagerie, each member of which has a right to have her needs addressed and, if possible to have her play needs fulfilled. (p. 242)

Thus to understand our children's play needs and better provide for them, an evolutionary perspective on playtypes would probably be very helpful.

Examining this evolving *neuroludic-evolutionary* model, through the prism of playwork and playwork values may also be productive. Earlier I suggested that different playtypes may have a physiological impact on the construction of different areas of the brain. Might it be that different playtypes facilitate the construction of specific neural areas? By this I mean, that for the child to be able to engage in locomotor play, for example, may have neurological implications for the genesis of synapses and cells in three separate and distinct brains, as proposed by MacLean. I am suggesting that this is in effect a neuroludic-evolutionary process. This forms a major theme throughout this book.

Thus MacLean's triune model raises serious implications for the development of effective and above all ethical, playwork practice. For it now falls to playworkers to ensure that the children they work with:

- not only have access to holistic playtypes experiences, that may mean, reptilian, limbic and neocortical experiences;
- not only have access to 'triune' play experiences, but that these are balanced between ALL of the different playtypes, to ensure appropriate growth in each of the three brains.

In this context it is critical that playworkers are not drawn into making spurious playtypes choices for children's neural development for educational or social reasons. For example, that access to one playtype is more important than another, or that a particular playtype, like rough and tumble is 'anti-social'. The child's right to play, means that *children alone* should make the play choices that will affect them. There is huge and frightening potential for the manipulation of the individual child or groups of children for personal and political, rather than biological, ends.

Conclusion

Given all that has been said, I am obliged to conclude that applying what we know about playtypes does seem to have far more mileage than I originally envisaged. This is particularly the case when I place them within the context of an evolving neuroludic-evolutionary construct. Within this theoretical notion using playtypes to ensure that the children with whom we work have balanced access to all types of survival and developmental experience is a crucial element of our informed practice. Ensuring that playspaces are not only diverse but continually evolving is another lesson I have drawn from these reflections. Ensuring the *triune nature of play experiences* may be another consideration in our practice. Forecasting adaptive trends and diagnosing disorders from potential playtypes mutations remains a serious piece of research for the future.

The question it all raises is where does this leave us as professional practitioners active in the child's playing? The short answer is: I can only make informed guesses. I said at the beginning that I only created the Taxonomy to solve a problem I saw at the time. But, life is rarely that straightforward and now we have lots of new questions to answer, some of which feel quite important. Answering them might be the first priority.

The remainder of this book is my attempt to do precisely that and to throw a little more light on my own perceptions of the phenomena of playtypes and their relevance and importance in playwork.

Chapter Two

What follows is a very partial analysis of the origins of playwork's theoretical base including playtypes. My memory of playwork's early years has decayed, and what follows might not be absolutely factual, although I think it is fairly accurate. Perhaps it would be best to read it and then talk to others about what they remember. Normally, mention of National Organisations applies to England only for simplicity. Scotland has Play Scotland, Northern Ireland, PlayBoard and Wales, PlayWales.

Origins

Although *A Playworker's Taxonomy of PlayTypes* was not written until 1996, knowledge of different types of play had been building in the psychological literature for many years prior to that. By the late 1970s, various types of play had been referred to in numerous publications. For example, entire books had been devoted to Symbolic Play.

However, in playwork during the 1960s and 70s, much of this was not in common usage. Neither had there been a perceived need or demand to know. Playworkers, the term mainly used to describe those who ran adventure playgrounds, all knew what each other meant when they talked about play, whilst their managers and funders did not appear interested in play as a phenomenon at all. Rather they were much more concerned about the numbers attending provision and on the effectiveness of play provision in tackling crime and other social issues.

Through their own observations and personal experience, playworkers knew that children played in numerous ways, some of which were physical and energetic, whilst others were more creative, or social or elemental, but that was as far as their analysis went. Instead they concentrated on creating, stocking and operating the environments, whilst the children played.

The absence of any formal analysis did not mean that playworkers were not interested in understanding play further. It was just that they already had their own internal 'folk' analysis of what was happening when children played and for then it sufficed. For many the prevailing analysis was rooted in left-wing politics, whilst for others a more biological analysis was beginning to emerge, but it was as romantic as it was scientific.

A sign that 'folk' analyses, whatever their foci, would not be sufficient in the climate of future change, came in the early 1980s when a number of good adventure playgrounds were closed by the local authorities who funded them. Whilst the funders argued that the closure of these adventure playgrounds was necessary because they were dangerous, dirty, unsightly and noisy, the playground's advocates were signally unable to argue competently a more positive alternative; the reason being that they had neither a theoretical base, nor a technical language to articulate a position that would render them capable of clearly and convincingly arguing why provision was needed, even though they probably knew why well enough. This inability to be able to convince non-playworkers of the importance of play and of provision for it, posed a serious challenge to playwork; a challenge that was to remain for some years.

The lack of ability to articulate a convincing basis for playwork was partially responsible for an appallingly low professional self-image in the playwork field. During the late 1970s and early 1980s, many playworkers felt inferior to other professional colleagues, their Youth and Social Work counterparts in particular. Many playworkers were low paid, some worked alone for long hours, often in all weathers, and most risked or experienced violent attacks from alienated children and young people. They were also expected to provide some kind of 'successful' service to local children, often without the necessary physical resources, budgets or professional support.

Unsympathetic social workers could be punitive when they interfaced with playworkers in those early days. Of course, they could have been forgiven for not understanding what playwork was, or what it was for – playworkers had enough problems articulating that themselves – but this common ground was all too often lost under the inflexible application of a relative blizzard of regulation, where previously there had been almost none. Understandably, playworkers felt powerless, and when opportunities arose for them to talk to others about what they did as a job, public speaking inexperience and professional frustration often combined to produce a torrent of unhelpful emotional outpouring.

However, this situation was not to last, and developments that would help to change it were already afoot. Whilst the adventure playground closures went ahead, the National Playing Fields Association – then the lead body for play provision and playwork in the UK – published an analysis of play and playwork in their magazine *PlayTimes*. This analysis was rooted in basic psychological, neurological and neurochemical premises and attempted to provide the embryo of a theoretical foundation for playwork intervention. The articles, which were written by two playworkers, and published over five issues, argued that play had proven bio-evolutionary roots, that play deprivation was an insidious menace and that good play provision and playwork could do much to facilitate comprehensive play experiences and combat the effects of play deprivation. It drew from numerous sources that were all cited and referenced – old hat now, but unusual then.

Response to the articles was muted at the time, but over the years they generated a lot of interest, and that continues up to the present day. The language used by playworkers to describe playwork methods and ideas also seemed to take on a more technical/

scientific bent from around that time, although whether the articles were in any way responsible for this is hard to say. However, the general point needs to be made that a specific playwork discourse was beginning to emerge.

Other evidence of a gradual shift in the acceptance of the need for a theoretical view of playwork came at around the same time, when a definition of play drawn exclusively from the literature was approved by the JNCTP, the Joint National Committee for Training in Playwork. This meant that it became the field's official definition of play, when prior to this there had not been one single agreed definition. Playwork training courses that were beginning to spring up also began to stress the importance for playwork practice of understanding play as a biological process, a process which had a role in the development of important skills such as communication, aesthetics and problem-solving.

The mid-1980s also witnessed another situation that again reinforced the importance for playwork to have a more integrated and relevant body of knowledge and a credible theoretical base. Around 1986, playwork experienced a sizeable influx of women and men from employment schemes. By then unemployment in the UK had reached double figures in terms of percentage of the population. Obviously, some of these people came into the work with values and aspirations quite different to those that had underpinned playwork for over a decade and a half.

This had the effect of highlighting how vulnerable playwork was at that time and how vital was the development of a theoretical base clarifying the uniqueness and integrity of playwork. Child-care, although a hugely contentious ethical and moral issue for many playworkers, was in the ascendancy. It was growing in leaps and bounds, was clearly a service that parents seemed to want and need, and child-care facilities were proliferating everywhere, whilst playwork budgets were being capped and cut.

Although later accused by some in the child-care lobby of being 'precious' and narrow in focus, playworkers held the view that playwork and child-care were not, and could not be, the same thing;

that whilst child-care was a 'business' driven by the needs and requirements of working parents, playwork was a compensatory 'bio-evolutionary' service to children. One that was driven not by economics or politics but by health backed by science, i.e. that children needed to play and that if they did not they would suffer serious harm. The scientific underpinning to support this assertion was still continuing to evolve, but playwork itself was in a chaotic state.

During the 1980s and early 1990s, national organisations created by government to promote and manage play and playwork in England came and went. First the National Playing Fields Association closed its Children and Youth Department to make way for the government-funded quango, The Association for Children's Play and Recreation Ltd. – the original PlayBoard. Then the ACPR Ltd., which had been created in 1984 as a response to the inner city riots of the early 80s, also closed. Then the NCPRU, The National Children's Play and Recreation Unit that was created in its place, went the same way. PlayCare, an odd mutation of playwork and child-care, was stillborn. Later in the 80s playwork in England became managed by the Sports Council, and then SPRITO (Sport, Playwork and Recreation Industry Training Organisation) was born and along with it the NVQ. Virtually overnight, playwork began to be described by some as part of leisure (of which another was 'caravans') within an 'industry', where presumably playwork would be just another job, play just another commodity, and children just another sector of consumers.

This was a very low point. Suddenly, much of playwork's agenda was being decided politically, but not through discussion with playworkers. Again, the lack of a fully articulated technical language and philosophy was obvious.

Nor was all the damage coming from external sources. During the same period, playwork was also being expected, by forces both from within and without, to contort itself to accommodate every aspect of the emerging community politics of the day – as well as being what it was, it also had to demonstrate that it was multi-culturalist, non-sexist, non-racist, non-sexual orientationist or genderist. It had to condemn bullying and discrimination of any and every kind and embrace equal opportunities.

The problem was that much of this forced reorientation was an adulteration, and contradicted the nature of life in a children's play environment, where more ancient currents had to coexist with those of more contemporary times. Playworkers had always mediated disputes, had always protected the oppressed and supported the disadvantaged – all children had the right to experience play – but the playworkers' input had to be made in ways that respected the play environment as the children's space first and foremost. If that were not the first premise then playworkers became the bully, the racist and the sexist, for forcing their views upon a whole raft of children often coming from different populations, belief systems and cultures. But for some years the new politics prevailed, and further developments of playwork theory and practice went on hold as the field looked to this new agenda for its training and direction.

In 1989 the Children Act arrived in England. This piece of legislation was so prescriptive in terms of staff/child ratios and child/toilet ratios that it looked like it would succeed where years of underfunding, professional suicidal tendencies and the horrendously difficult task of attempting to create a new discipline had not. Now playwork justifiably feared for its very existence. The Children Act moved playwork spaces into the legislative strictures of a primary school. In some ways this was motivated by genuine concern, but it completely contradicted the reality of play for children in the wild and, as a consequence, could have had the effect of negating some, if not all, of the benefits of playing.

Light at the end of the tunnel

However, rumours of the demise of play and playwork proved premature. Children still wanted to play, parents too still wanted their children to play and Local Authorities around the country still insisted on making provision, including adventure playgrounds run by playworkers. Except now, they had to wrestle with satisfying the

Children Act legislation. However, even this was made easier by negotiations held between PLAYLINK, a charity that grew from the London Adventure Playground Association and the Department of Health, the department from which the legislation had been derived.

Universities and Colleges throughout the UK had now begun to proliferate and diplomas, degrees and MAs in playwork became available. The NVQ pathway was exposing large numbers of potential playworkers to playwork's ideas and practices. For the first time there were probably more people studying playwork than there were in its practice.

However, with all the different playwork courses and learning opportunities that were becoming available, the danger now became that playwork would become 'all things to all people' and that each country, region, university or college in the UK, would have its own completely different interpretation of what playwork was.

As with every other discipline, to some extent this was unavoidable, but because of the prevailing legislative, funding and professional context there was legitimate concern that without what Sturrock later called a 'North', playwork could still lose its focus on play, and instead find itself straying into child-care, homework and special activity clubs. If for no other reason than that increasingly was where the money lay. It was felt that one major defence against this incursion was to have more written about what playwork was trying to address in its practice.

At the time, most libraries in those academic institutions offering playwork courses had a sizeable and authoritative collection of *play* literature, but their collections of material from *playwork* was neither sizeable nor particularly authoritative. One reason for this was that relative to play, little had still been written about playwork. This meant that material that enabled playworkers and student playworkers better to understand the rationale and knowledge base from which playwork had evolved, and was continuing to evolve, still had to be created. One development that should have been more significant than actually transpired was the launch in 1993 of the *International Play Journal*. Intended to be an international platform for the debate of playwork's theory and practice, it closed in 1996.

We have now reached 1994/5 and after working for the NPFA, running PlayEducation, and working on three adventure playgrounds, I was then working for PLAYLINK as its Training Manager.

I am one of those who, throughout the periods documented above, had been attempting to capture and document various parts of what I saw as playwork's underpinning ideas and practices. At some point during my time at PLAYLINK, I became aware of the confusion of certain terminology being used to describe play, in a number of the publications of the day. The problem was that descriptions of the social contexts, within which play was taking place, were themselves being passed off as play. For example, descriptors such as cooperative, solitary and parallel, were being used alongside descriptions of play that could be found in the literature, for example, rough and tumble and locomotor.

Not a huge issue on the face of it, but unclear thinking that concerned me and one that I felt should be addressed. At the suggestion of PLAYLINK's Director, Sandra Melville, and to avoid any further confusions and inaccuracies about what was play and what was not, I set about researching and writing a categorisation of play sub-divisions as a tool for playworkers. The result was *A Playworker's Taxonomy of PlayTypes*. It was published by PLAYLINK in 1996.

About the Taxonomy

Much of 1995 I spent in libraries searching for material that identified different kinds of play.

Predictably, some of what I uncovered was already known to me and I imagine to most of the playwork field. There were numerous accounts of girls playing with dolls and boys fighting, of children pretending to be horses and trees and of children and other species manipulating objects and engaging in a sensory exploration of their world.

However, as time passed, and as I became increasingly immersed in the literature, I found myself becoming more drawn into a search for what I felt was 'real play', play that I had seen daily on the playground. Raw play, as manifested in intense, dynamic, vibrant, authentic, dangerous and urgent interactions with the world. Of course, like their researched counterparts, the children I had worked with also played with dolls, wrestled, imagined and manipulated, but the research literature described the children and the events in that sterile style symptomatic of research. The context for playwork was not like that, a point that was frequently made when playworkers had the opportunity to talk to their academic colleagues in psychology, and other related areas.

With a few notable exceptions, Robin Moore's, *Childhood's Domain*, for example, which is essentially anecdotal and qualitative, the literature continued to frustrate my search to locate the vibrant core of what I knew existed on the playground and was happening to the children I had worked with. The real play I had observed engaged children in the passions of hate and love, rendered them violent and gentle, made them take unbelievable risks, and created heroes who cried and were afraid of the dark. The children I worked with believed in devils, myths and rituals, they could be both cruel and forgiving, so different to the 'stiff' children depicted in the laboratory studies.

Where was this in the literature? Where was play in the raw? Or was I just romanticising or imagining what I thought I had observed?

Imagine my delight and relief when I discovered Clifford Geertz's essay on 'Deep Play'. Instantly, I recognised it as my 'real play'. It took play onto its proper level, a dignified level, a level of worth. It took matters onto a level I knew both intuitively *and* from experience. As a term, *Deep* Play, described what I had done myself as a child, whether that was giving voice to small toys, frightening myself with my own imaginings, peering into death or sex, taking risks with heights, roads, trains and iced-up flooded rivers, engaging in combat, or simply being awestruck by the realisation of where we all are and the feelings of overwhelming insignificance and gut-crunching beauty I had, when looking at the night sky from my bedroom window.

But although it had this generic interpretation, it also focussed on one particular aspect of playing. Certainly, there is this profound sense in which all play is deep, but in my personal childhood experience, some play was deeper, more scary, more ominous than others.

Going into underground drainage tunnels, where you had to depend upon your friends and your non-visual senses, felt like we were interfacing with death itself. They were just so dark and strange, and sometimes a wood or an allotment would be so silent, or alternatively full of the sounds of the wind. These experiences would manifest the feelings of loneliness and powerlessness, which made us feel we were in the company of something otherworldly. We did not engage in these experiences so that we would actually die, or would really encounter ghosts, but so that we would continue to push our experience beyond its normal limits; almost like playing to mature. As it also seemed so tangled up with the notion of the paranormal or the metaphysical, Deep Play also provided a route for us into a kind of child 'spirituality', which I wrote about in a little story entitled 'Caves'. The more one 'pushed the limit' the more one felt equipped to reflect upon deeper issues. Of course, we also all frightened each other to death.

Importantly though, the term 'Deep Play' seemed to encapsulate much of the day-to-day play reality of the children who came to the playgrounds I had operated.

I believe that for most children life is tough in one way or another. This is inevitably reflected in how they engage with the universe when they play, as what they play at passes through the prism of how they feel. Play is not always the pleasant experience some would have us believe. It can be chaotic, it can be physically painful, it can contain rejection, it can also contain fear and panic. So the term Deep Play is both an acknowledgement and a manifestation of the level at which life can be conducted and perceived by children when they are playing; that the play life of children includes much the same dark-side, or shadow, as does adult life.

The problem with play as depicted in the laboratory is that, except in exceptional therapeutic contexts, it does not show this depth. It does not even suggest or indicate its existence. All too often, it seems to provide an edited version of what the adult researchers remember their play being like. Although this can yield interesting insights, it only provides a part of the picture one observes in real life, a picture that knowledge of Deep Play can help to complete.

The human world children are entering is, as well as many other things, cruel, violent, exploitative, sexual and greedy. It would be odd if the embryonic proto-tendencies of these human components were not reflected in what children played at, or in how they played.

I was, therefore, delighted to discover Deep Play in the literature. It reassured me that the science would be comprehensive and balanced. Until then I had been concerned that that would not be the case and that only 'permissible', i.e. polite, play would be admissible in the discourse.

One of the other play manifestations I was relieved to find described was 'Mastery Play'. I doubt if there is a child on the planet who has not engaged, or wanted to engage in, mastery play, particularly at the seaside or on the riverbank.

Like 'Deep Play', 'Mastery Play' was one of the other kinds of play that one saw on the playground all the time. This may have been because it was allowed in these spaces, whereas it may have been regarded as a prohibited form of behaviour by parents and carers. Children were always digging, creating tunnel and bridge worlds in sand, and pitting themselves against the environment and the elements. Even though these two kinds of play are often very visible, I think they have very different roots. Deep Play is pessimistic, almost an acknowledgement of eventual mortality – of playing with mortality, as it states in the Taxonomy – whereas

Mastery Play is quite the reverse. It is optimistic, more an arrogant refusal on the part of the child to accept that s/he is not all-powerful and omnipotent.

A Taxonomy of PlayTypes?

At the end of the research period for the Taxonomy I had identified fifteen kinds of play that had been referred to consistently in the literature. And these were to became the basis of my taxonomy of …?

Now, I was left with the problem of what to call them. For some time I had felt that kinds of play should be referred to as play 'modes'. Having read so much about them, they felt as if they expressed different ways of being – they were certainly different ways of acting or doing, as 'mode' is defined in the dictionary. But a mode, particularly in the context of a behavioural sequence, seemed to describe something much more complex than the material I had collected suggested to me at that time. To call them 'modes' implied a knowledge of the intricacy of different ways of playing and I certainly did not have then this understanding and, more importantly, it appeared neither did anyone else.

Play fighting, for example, although easily recognised, involves a very complicated collection of movements, pressures and decisions, which when run together, can be identified as play fighting. We can recognise the sum total of what constitutes play fighting even though we are less than clear about the various components.

Consequently, I decided to avoid the term play 'modes', thinking that perhaps it could be revisited when we knew more about what a 'mode' might contain. I opted instead for the less definitive play 'type': a term that implied that we were able to distinguish between what appeared to be different behavioural modes, but that was all. For many, even the breakdown of play into its component 'types' has proved a difficult sub-division.

So, the manual became *A Taxonomy of PlayTypes*. Each type occupied its own section and each section was broken down into parts entitled – The Name and Alternative Name/s of that Type; What the

Literature Says (here were included a selection of quotes from the literature); Playwork Comments (these were playwork observations on that particular playtype); Examples and Ideas for Modification (which made suggestion about how environments could be adapted to facilitate the various playtypes). Each section also had playful examples of that playtype, supplied by two experienced playworkers, Mick Conway and Jess Milne.

The updated second edition published in 2002 added a small 'indicators' section for each playtype too. This was included to help playworkers identify each individual playtype, as it was displayed by children, in their playing.

The importance of the scientific underpinning

That each of the playtypes had been located in, and drawn from, the literature was important for the authority of the Taxonomy. For some years playwork had been attempting to use scientific findings to support its own developing theory. The scientific world had the opportunity and resources to study play, which playwork did not, and now that was being realised.

For example, in the introduction to the first edition the suggestion was put forward that each 'type' described a unique way of interfacing with mind or environment:

> Whilst the reason different 'play types' might exist remains unknown, one possible explanation might be that each playtype is a specific biological 'key' to a different 'treasure chest' of knowledge and understanding in the environment and that only by playing in a particular way can we unlock the knowledge to which that 'key' applies. (p. 2)

(This paragraph is written slightly differently in the second edition.)

This was an interesting and apparently rather controversial idea for playwork, for it implied that children could only experience the full range of what playing offered if they regularly engaged in all fifteen playtypes. The idea was that each playtype was so discrete, so individual and so unique, both in terms of movement and neural consequences, that the access it offered to certain information, feelings, and neural processes could not be overlapped or represented by experience of another, perhaps similar, type.

The reasoning was simple. If playtypes were the result of the evolutionary process, natural selection would not tolerate the existence of two different playtypes that did the same things: one would have been selected out. Of course there may have been similarities in how some types were perceived by adults, but my assertion was that each playtype was so different internally that its benefits could not be replicated by engaging in any of the others. I still believe this, and to some extent this has been borne out by more recent discoveries. For example, Burghardt (1998) states that play is 'most certainly' a heterogeneous category and that different types of play may have 'different causal bases, functions, phylogenies and ontogenies' (p. 6).

The 'suggestion' made in the first edition was intended to stimulate serious questions about the kinds of environments that were being proposed for children's play. Many of the varieties of play environments, particularly the 'fixed equipment spaces', traditionally on offer to children, could only cater for a modicum of the playtypes contained in the Taxonomy.

Perhaps the most important playwork conclusion that came from the Taxonomy was that if the fifteen playtypes were seen as a behavioural range, and that if each of the playtypes was seen as a possible spectrum of actions, rather than as one specific routine, then collectively playtypes could be seen as facilitating and underpinning most of how we engage with, and describe, the universe. Playtypes as a concept are so comprehensive that I find it impossible to imagine any that are missing.

Except one!

In the second edition, I decided to add a playtype to the list that already existed. It was 'Recapitulative Play'.

I had always maintained that the Taxonomy was work in

progress. The sub-division of play into 'types' was likely to be relatively arbitrary and, until a great deal more research had been done, was bound to remain so. The Taxonomy was always intended as a tool rather than an unchanging icon, so the second edition should be seen as the first in a series of updates.

By the second edition, I had been exploring 'recapitulation' as a play/playwork idea for some years and was becoming increasingly convinced that 'recapitulation' as discussed by G. Stanley Hall and Reaney, might in some way be related to the new science of 'epigenetics', where aspects of experience from the past had been genetically inherited by generations in the future. Hall's Recapitulation Theory implied that genetic inheritance could go back many thousands of years.

Expanding on the work of Hall, Mabel Reaney (1916) proposed that the various stages of childhood could be divided into 'play periods' that corresponded with man's various evolutionary stages. For example 'the animal stage ... the savage stage ... the nomad stage ... the pastoral stage and the tribal stage' (Schwartzman 1978, p. 47).

I wondered: If 50 or 100 years, or even ten thousand, why not to the beginning of our evolution?

Although I appreciated that much of epigenetic thinking is at the cutting edge of science, it seemed reasonable to ask: If old or even ancient genetic information *is* being transferred through the generations and inherited by each of them, why is this happening and how is this information being activated? After all, it is possible given our evolution that old information and relatively more modern information may have been encoded differently. Do we do something that unifies genetic information into one code?

My response to the former was straightforward. Over the millions of years of our evolution we have adapted to a whole variety of conditions. This adaptation has kept the ever present pressures of extinction at bay. It seems rational, given that our survival would be at stake, that not only would we generate a mechanism for memorising that information, but that we would also find some way of passing it on for the benefit of each generation to come. This would incrementally include their own contribution. All that remained would be for the evolutionary process to select the appropriate mechanism. This would explain why *epigenetic recapitulation* occurred. (I am not claiming to be an expert on epigenetics, but this forms an interesting hypothetical working title.) However, the process of recapitulation is a key component of the construct of neuroludic-evolutionary theory.

More important from a playwork perspective was the question: How is this information being activated?

In the past few years I have been exposed through the literature to the notion of 'sensitive periods'. One description of this phenomenon particularly struck me.

> Play must represent a sensitive period during which the performance of certain motor patterns can alter development. A well-known example of such development occurs in many songbirds, in which a young bird must perform the motor act of singing (subsong) to modify the structure of the neurons that issue motor commands for singing. (Byers 1998, p. 208)

What I understood this to mean was that during a sensitive period of which play is one, if certain predefined sub-movements are undertaken, brain change is brought about that makes more complicated processes, like singing, happen.

I wondered if play's sensitive period had a role in 'turning on' or even in 'de-coding' genetic information. Hall and Reaney had both discussed children recapitulating or recapping their evolutionary history, but neither had offered a satisfactory reason why this should happen. If engaging in recapitulation was the human equivalent of the songbird's subsong, then perhaps the purpose of recapitulation was that by engaging in the structural modification, genetic information, including ancient genetic information that had been passed on to the next generation, but which was unactivated, became activated and useable.

In short, what I was proposing was that children engage in 'reca-pitulative play' because by so doing they both 'decode' and 'turn-on', genetic information from the past. (*Examples of the kinds of play experiences that would be manifested during recapitulative play are given in Chapter Three.*)

The idea of 'recapitulative play' fascinated me enough to 'float' the idea in the second edition of the Taxonomy, and it has certainly exercised many minds. Whether it remains in the third edition is really down to the field's continued response.

Benefits of a knowledge of playtypes

Magic and Non-Magic

Perhaps one of the more practical benefits that stems from a categorisation of playtypes is that it better enables an interface between the two systems that Sturrock (2004), paraphrasing Goertzel (1993), called Magician and Anti-Magician Systems. I am adapting Sturrock's terminology further to create what is hopefully an intelligible paradigm for playwork, the Magic and Non-Magic System.

Many of those who make the existence of provision for children possible, live in professional circumstances, which at least on the face of it, have to be much more rational than those where good playwork takes place. Looking after budgets, being sensitive to legislation, interfacing with the national and local political reality, all require of Local Government Officers and those who run equiv-alent organisations to have, at least at work, a non-emotional, and certainly a non-mystical approach to what they do. They have to exist in what might be called a Non-Magic System. Often, as a conse-quence they may find it difficult to understand or even value the perceptions or the language of those who do not.

Playworkers, on the other hand exist in what might be termed a Magic System, in which rationality is only a small part of the neces-sary professional application and culture.

The play environment is a unique and often strange place, where, because its primary population is children, many of whom are passing through early and middle childhood, the products of the different playtypes, fantasy, imagination, metaphysical insights and mastery, are what constitutes their most immediate reality.

Expectations are different from what I term, 'the world beyond the wire'. Because they are in a continuum of 'the absorption of understanding' children shock the adult observer in many ways, not only with their dexterity, athleticism, absence of fear, and sophistication of language and reason, but with the mysterious way in which they interface with one another and the play space itself. As well as the children, the playworker is also immersed in this 'reality of fantasy' and it has a huge affect upon playworker protocols, whereas for the others I mention, their professional protocol is instead immersed in 'fantasy of reality' and those protocols are also affected as a consequence.

These are by necessity very different takes on reality, and it is not surprising that difficulties can arise. However, one of the great benefits of a categorisation like the Taxonomy is that, irrespective of professional perspective, it does give individuals from both systems the opportunity to communicate through something about which they both have personal experience. It provides 'common ground' upon which an understanding of perceptions and thinking can take place, even though those perceptions may be very different and differently articulated.

After all, play is play. Everyone, irrespective of the part they play in creating provision, will have an understanding and experience of it and, therefore, a stake in what is provided and why it needs to be there. Playtypes enable discussion to take place at a level that perhaps, until the development of the Taxonomy, had not been possible between these two very different systems.

Analysis and diagnosis

Once, playwork's perception of play was relatively simple. In the last decade and a half increasing scientific knowledge and theoretical playwork speculation have advanced that perception considerably. When something as complex as our contemporary model of play, is simply referred to, globally, as play, very little can be said further about it. However, once the term is broken down into its component parts, we can then explore them further. We can find out the patterns that construct them and examine those patterns for gaps or new developments.

The phenomenon of play could be evolving new playtypes. How would we know? Old playtypes may be decaying or disappearing altogether. How too would we know that? Only by studying play, becoming fluent in identifying and analysing playtypes, might we begin to understand the mystery of play; what it is and what it is for.

In the same way that an understanding of chromosomes and genetics is revealing how some human conditions exist and what might be done to alleviate their effects, just so a greater understanding of play mechanics might enable us to understand better whether the extended or reduced routines in play modes that may be manifested on the playground, constitute a risk to children's well-being or not.

About this book

PlayTypes – Speculations and Possibilities is not an extension or an upgrade of the *Playworker's Taxonomy*. Whilst this book revisits the playtypes categorised in the Taxonomy, to provide a bit more substance to what has already been written, its real purpose is to use the original Taxonomy as a springboard for a deeper exploration of what playtypes might be for and how that theoretical journey might better inform our practice.

Since the original Taxonomy was developed, our knowledge about the relationship between play and neurological development, in particular, has moved on considerably and this has made it possible to pose important and interesting questions that relate to playwork practice and playtypes.

It is a theoretical speculation, which attempts to unpick what playworkers observe children doing on a daily basis and put it into a framework that enables us better to explain what the role of play-types is in the development of behaviour.

Chapter Three

Each playtype is both distinctly and subtly different from each of the others. From a playwork perspective it is useful to be able to recognise each one and be able to distinguish between them. One reason why this is useful, is that engaging in each one is a necessary corollary for a child's healthy development. We need to know that children are engaging in them all, or at least that they can, if they so choose. This has practical implications for us. For, if children are not engaging in the whole range of the playtypes that have been identified, is this because they choose not to, or because they cannot because the whole range is not available, or is something else stopping them that we should know about and perhaps address?

Playworkers need to be continually monitoring the environment and the children for evidence that the materials, loose parts and ambiance (props), needed for them to engage in each of the playtypes are available and that children are taking up this engagement.

What follows is an observed and instinctive, rather than an academic, guide to recognising all sixteen playtypes.

Identifying PlayTypes – Some Basic Characteristics

Irrespective of a child's culture, their geographic location, their gender or any disability they might have, the playtypes routines in which that child engages show certain general characteristics. These are shared by every other child and are as beautiful as they are awe-inspiring.

For example, we recognise a behavioural routine as a PlayType when it shows the following characteristics:

Species Unity – A oneness of the fundamental origins of all children, irrespective of perceived differences.

Symmetry of Expression – Each playtype always conforms to its categorical description. For example, rough and tumble play can be recognised uniformly in that category. However, within certain descriptive parameters, irrespective of who is manifesting them and where, there are variations, which may be geographical, cultural, and so forth.

Uniformity of Purpose – Whilst little about playtypes can be 'proved', the literature does suggest that 'at the very least' they are involved in brain and muscle growth. I would go further and suggest that each playtype has a specific function (perhaps in constructing a particular neural area) irrespective of who is engaging in it.

Fluidity of Merge, Exchange or Interchange – Each playtype can merge effortlessly with every other playtype. Each playtype can be effortlessly interchanged for every other playtype. Each playtype can merge with all aspects of the 'whole' environment.

Infinite Capacity for 'Fit' – This is a subset of Fluidity of Merge and refers to the capacity of each playtype to 'fit' or 'adapt' itself to the format that follows on from it, irrespective of whether that format is manifested by its host child, an adjacent child, or a feature of the physical/psychological environment.

Utilisation of Affect – Playtypes do not have a specific emotional signature of their own; rather they can be displayed in any emotional context.

Multi-faceted Application Interface – Playtypes have the capacity to interact with any medium. They have no specific home or time.

Phylogenetic Expression – In different circumstances, playtypes will manifest themselves according to the phylogenetic address activated by the fusion of that playtype and the circumstances in which it is being activated.

(*See Chapter Seven for further discussion and examples.*)

Multi-Adaptive Potential – Each playtype offers its own versions of this potential. When a playtype is activated, what we can see is an adaptive approximation. What this means, is when the child summons up a particular playtype, in say, Manchester, what we see is what is manifested in Manchester's conditions. As a biological mechanism, this has fundamental uses: if in other conditions, Australian or Japanese for example, the same playtype is manifested with minute adaptive variations, it may act to facilitate adaptation to those particular conditions.

For example, Social Play as a basic playtype description can be generated, to a greater or lesser extent, in modes of social interaction that will cross cultures, economic orders, geographical zones and varying climatic conditions. Locomotor Play as a basic playtype description can be generated in modes of three-dimensional movement that can address the locomotor challenges of any terrain that exists on earth.

Identifying PlayTypes – General Descriptions

Playtypes are manifested in sixteen different forms that range from three-dimensional movement to rough and tumble, and from exploration of, and experimentation with, objects and spaces, to dialogue and symbolism. What follows is intended to provide further insights into what to look for.

Communication Play

If the playworker cannot detect the sounds of talking, conversation, shouting, singing, name calling, swearing, laughing, jokes or arguing, then given that the play space is a space that children inhabit and that communication play is highly prolific, this would be thought of as rather odd, unless the children were being told a story, or other forms of quiet interchange were taking place. Normally, the play space would be ringing with the noises that their interaction would generate. For example, think of a family with two or three children and the amount of noise they can generate and then imagine that multiplied twenty or thirty times. For many adults, this barrage of sound is something they find both painful and intimidating, and quite difficult to cope with, particularly in an enclosed indoor space. But for the playworker, the level of happy noise, and the hustle and bustle that usually goes with it, is a good indicator of the success or otherwise of the project.

High quality Communication Play is not for the prude or for the naturally repressive. Children's language, jokes and songs can be filthy and repellent. I remember my own experiments with expletives, innocently trying them out at the dinner table!

An eight-year-old child I was at school with created my favourite rhyme. We were both in the same class, and our teacher, Mr Carr, had asked us to write a poem. This is what my friend wrote:

> Mr Carr, had a car,
> He drove into a public bar,
> A copper come, and smacked his bum,
> Ha, Ha, Ha.

A rhyme we all knew and which also appeared at around the same time was:

Little Robin Red Breast sat upon a pole, cocked up his right leg and showed his little ...
Old Mother Reilly had a fat cow, how to milk it she didn't know

how, she pulled its tail instead of its tit, and all she got was a
lump of ...

Ships on the ocean made of brass, ever see a monkey licking its ...

Ask no questions tell no lies, ever seen a policeman doing up
his ...

Flies are a nuisance, bugs are worse, and that is the end of my
little verse.

One which was directed at one of my own group of friends was,

Ed, Ed, shit the bed, told his Mother he laid an egg, when his
Mother came to look, she stuck her finger in the poop.

But Communication Play is not just verbal. Children are signalling
their intentions, their feelings and judgements to one another all the
time. They shrug their disinterest; they sit angrily; they smile or
glare, depending on how they feel about the recipient. From an early
age they generate and collect a whole armoury of sophisticated non-
verbal interfaces that are intended to communicate everything from,
'I like you', to 'You make me sick', and from 'I feel lonely', to 'That
tasted vile'. They use everything from eyes, whole faces, tongue,
hands, head and eye movements, to how they sit, stand and walk, to
convey the complex nuances and emphases that are the currency of
communication.

Everything is tried and explored for effect, for what works and
how well it works. 'If I say it this way, nothing happens. But if I say
it this way, and at the same time stand like this, kids back off and
appear intimidated', or alternatively, 'they act as if they like me'.

Communication Play is essentially very rich as a source of play
cues. The play face, reported by Bateson (1955) and van Hooff
(1972), can take an infinite number of forms that depend upon
minute or more gross changes of forehead, eyes, lips, mouth, nose,
and combinations thereof, for their transmission. Yet all of them
give the message, to varying degrees, 'I want to play', or 'this is
play'. In terms of their diversity of potency, look at the effect of

sticking out the tongue while smiling, for example. Whilst both components may work as a cue, neither the smile, nor the tongue being stuck out alone, has quite the provocative impact as both have together. So if a child wants to be chased, that's the face to use.

To identify Communication Play, we need to look for changes in posture and face, we need to look for touching or gestures, and we need to listen for auditory signals like words or sounds, all or some of which are being directed at a recognisable, although not necessarily a human or live recipient.

Creative Play

The essence of Creative Play is in its drive to generate flexible combinations and permutations of shapes, textures, colours, sounds, tastes and/or smells. It is the expression of the outward flow of the senses, after they have passed through the prism of feelings. The Creative Play drive can be activated wherever there are 'loose parts' (Nicholson 1971) to manipulate, paints to apply, materials to weave, mould and shape, sounds to make and wherever there are ideas or emotions to interpret. But it does help to have a creative ambiance too, where 'permission to experiment', is implicit, and where the range and type of available materials does not become narrow or predictable. The playworker can switch off as well as help to activate this playtype simply by being boring, and replacing the exciting with the mundane. One playworker I knew was the source of many creative opportunities. He would, I am told, often raid skips on his way to the playground, as a way of ensuring a constant and varying supply of unpredictable and surprising loose parts (Conway 2004).

Although there are some notable exceptions, I have to say that the ubiquitous Play Resource Centre could perhaps do more to support this playtype, instead of rendering what should be, in my opinion, an intermittent supply of potentially creative consumables – that in turn can be channelled by children into original expressions of local experience and emotion – into a reliable retail outlet, where the same choice and diversity is ever present. Where the skip raider was the scrap equivalent of the small shopkeeper, so some members of the current mutation of Resource Centres are in danger of becoming the equivalent of the hypermarket of scrap.

Having said that, there are still those that search out the 'novel', the 'rare', and the 'precious' to ensure that their authentic contribution to this playtype is sustained. At one of these outlets, for example, I saw fantastic constructions made from electrical resistors of varying sizes and colours.

Creative Play can be a solitary venture or a dynamic social experiment; children can be alone or in groups when they are so engaged. However, for this playtype to successfully play through each child, and be visible to the playworker, one criterion has to be satisfied, more than any other. That criterion is that the child must be in control.

For, however else creativity is facilitated, control of what, how and why something is created in the first place must be initiated by the child or the children involved. That even means that children should not be told to interact with creative materials in the first place.

Recently (2005), I observed a group of children involved in an arts and crafts activity, supported by a few adults. Noise and movement were minimal, and whatever else the children were experiencing, it was not control over what they were doing.

After a period of time, three sacks of assorted scrap materials and loose parts were emptied into a heap on the floor nearby. 'Shall we let the children go now?' asked one of the support adults. 'No,' I said. 'Leave them doing what they're doing, but you adults, come away.' The adults disengaged from what the children were doing and went to sit in another part of the room. Because the children were quite immersed in what they were doing, it took some time for them to 'surface' and realise that the adults were gone and that there was a pile of scrap on the floor. Initially, there was little interest in the scrap and loose parts. The children were almost reluctant. It is actually quite hard work to surface from an immersion only to immerse oneself again.

After just two or three minutes from the time the adults left, a child disengaged herself from the arts and crafts activity and went to look at the pile of materials on the floor and started slowly to engage in similar exploration. Her interaction must have energised some of the others who also walked over to the pile and began to explore it. Literally, within a few minutes, at least ten different creative episodes were being undertaken by the group, including making and using vehicles from boxes, creating a quiz game, playing pretend musical instruments and making a town from blocks and small toys. The children were vibrant, noisy, animated and authentically immersed, taking their play around the adults and out of the room.

Personal control is also an important feature of creative play when children are attracted to engage in activities that require application and practice, such as painting, pottery and playing musical instruments. I have advocated elsewhere (Hughes 1996b) that my preferred option for such activities is to invite professionals into play environs to do what they do. Not to teach or instruct but merely to be. In this way children become aware of the discipline and difficulty that can go hand in hand with creativity, if the artist wants to take what s/he does to a higher level. More importantly it gives the child the opportunity to study the activity from close quarters, to see how this person does it. Not, you understand, to see how it is done.

Children who have good play experiences know intuitively that there are many ways to do everything, but a part of their pre-application analysis is in assessing the difficulties for themselves. An understanding of skills helpful to creativity such as concentration, dexterity, focus, material relationship (i.e. the relationship the artist has with materials), breathing, balance, interpretation, colour and mood coordination, and perseverance, inform children not only about whether this is for them, but also about how to develop an entry strategy that enables them to engage on their terms, and how to begin to interface on the terms of the art form.

This 'graduated immersion' enables children to engage with

creativity emotionally as well as mechanically, and begin the process of externally representing internal processes.

To identify Creative Play, we should look for an active, imaginative and affective engagement with materials or loose parts, with colours and the tools of art, or with musical instruments, that is under the control and direction of the child.

Deep Play

Engaging in Deep Play is how children begin to understand and develop a power relationship with the psychic environment that surrounds them.

For the playworker the child's need to engage in Deep Play is probably the most difficult of all the playtypes to consider. Its very existence is a demonstration of the fragility and transitional nature of life itself. This impacts on playworker and child alike.

Engagement in Deep Play symbolises the child's desire to confront what s/he most fears, the human condition of mortality and death. However, to observe it, is also to acknowledge that the child (or those children) is expressing the one quality that has enabled the human species to continue to be, when the pressures of extinction should have made it otherwise. That quality is optimism, without which we would have capitulated to these pressures long ago. For what Deep Play is, is a journey into the 'shadow' with every intention of surviving.

Deep Play represents a very real journey on the part of every child who engages in it. Whether that journey includes standing up against a bully, climbing to a challenging height, swinging perilously close to solid objects, confronting a phobia, or simply throwing oneself into space and going down the aerial runway for the first time. In a sense, Deep Play should also be described in graduations: Deep Play 1, Deep Play 2, 3 and 4, and so on, because it is not the same experience over and over again. Deep Play 1, the child's first experience of Deep Play, is the most challenging and can for the first few times be equated with leaping over a metaphorical cliff. Although the risks are still there during later engagements –

Deep Play 2, 3 or 4 in a graduated operation – by then most children will have begun to accumulate skills to countermand these fears.

In my experience, it is very rare that children actually injure themselves when they engage in this playtype. They extend their limits gradually and are only looking to experience a representation rather than the reality of death or damage. When they do, it normally means that they have either been pushed by someone, or have pushed themselves significantly beyond their abilities. This possibility and its potential consequences should act as a serious reminder of the impact of peer pressure (or even playworker pressure), or the development of a culture between children in which they move past risk and engage in the foolhardy or potentially suicidal activity of the serial thrill-seeker.

However, perhaps what may be most valuable for the child about this playtype is that engaging in it not only gives children an interface with death and mortality; it also provides a route into contemplating the 'deeper' ideas associated with it: the 'meaning' of life, or better still, 'putting meaning to life'. This is the driving force for the realisation of, and continuation of, a conscious engagement with existence. Perhaps the 'deep', in Deep Play implies playing with a conceptual or abstract depth, as well as a physical depth.

However, I suspect that there is a predictable, addictive quality to Deep Play, given its own lethal potential and the temptation for many children, for many different reasons, to end it all. This is one reason why we should continually make an engagement in each of the other playtypes an attractive proposition for children. Bias towards any playtype could be unhealthy in some sense, but a bias towards Deep Play could eventually become life-threatening.

To identify Deep Play we should look for children attempting to engage with experiences for the first time. These would normally entail risky or demanding motion – such as complex swinging, climbing to height, balancing over drops, or unorthodox activity, such as riding a bike down a slide. Look for hesitancy and fear. Assess the playspace for Deep Play outlets. The more outlets, the more the playworker should be alert to children overextending themselves. Be conscious of, and monitor, children attempting to engage in activity out of the playworker's gaze.

Dramatic Play

There is sense in which some Dramatic Play is Fantasy or Imaginative Play but in a formal 'framed' setting. One fine example of Dramatic Play I have observed recently was a child holding a non-existent pistol (I'm guessing, of course), and using every other child in the play space as a potential target – hiding as they approached, tailing them, rolling to the left and right to avoid being seen. It was dramatic rather than imaginary, simply because the child was not only acting-out, realistically replicating moves he had seen in films or on TV, but he was also conscious of what he was doing and looked to his peers for recognition and acclamation.

Another good example that comes to mind was that of a group of children at a party engaging in the choreographed moves of a 'Girl Band' when the current hit single was being played by the DJ. This was also a replication of something 'real', an acting-out of a real routine. What made this a particularly powerful example for me, was that this was a party for children with 'learning disabilities', which in this context was a descriptive term of questionable accuracy. For these children were expert at studying, memorising and displaying complex dance moves, together with accompanying facial moves and body postures of the individuals being dramatised.

Performance and display are critical features to look for when identifying Dramatic Play. Children seem to love engaging in it anyway, but the icing on the cake is the audience. Another feature is the creation of what Else and Sturrock (1998) call a 'play frame'. In this case it could well be a physical, rather than an imagined frame for their Dramatic Play, a stage or enclosure within which their dramatic creation can unfold.

The other primary ingredient for Dramatic Play is of course, dressing-up, and making-up. Look for children wearing clothes for a role, for children whose facial features have been altered by make-up or face paints. Look for the creation of a frame or stage, and listen for new voices and look for new identities.

Finally, the exploration of identity as a concept, or of personal identity as an experiment, is a predictable but important corollary to Dramatic Play for children as they engage in it. It facilitates the expression of personal qualities that otherwise might remain hidden or suppressed, and because of this, Dramatic Play is a very liberating playtype.

Exploratory Play

In 2005 I worked with the playworkers at Toffee Park Adventure Playground in London, to develop and build a rope bridge suspended between two large structures. It was constructed specifically to facilitate games of off-ground tag, but it had a number of swing and climbing features and we forecast that children would create other uses for it.

What is fascinating about this kind of modification is that although experienced playworkers can predict how it is likely to be used to some extent, they are continually surprised by the ingenuity that children show as they explore the possibilities of such a structure. This is what Exploratory Play is all about. And as there is a sense in which all play is symbolic (Sturrock 2002), there is also a sense that all play is exploratory.

Where children engage with a recent modification – like the rope bridge mentioned above – if it contains secrets, hidden possibilities or potentials, they will discover them, sometimes immediately, sometimes over time.

For example, the bridge could bounce, it could swing sideways, it could be an intrinsic part of a game like tag, or a part of a wider narrative, like a bridge in the jungle, whilst other children would climb onto it and swing on its swings.

We often forget, because as adults we have lost interest to some extent, that children's experience of discovery is hugely affective. It is highly anticipatory, exciting and fulfilling to tease out new experience from the environment. It is only when the environment, or that particular feature of the environment is exhausted of what it has to offer, that new modification, which will yield new opportunities for exploration, is necessary.

We also forget that the gradually extending environmental ranging with which children engage also feels much more highly charged for them than it does for us. Each new vista is filled with awesome potential, each arc of the swing is a unique gravitational event, and every additional inch from the ground is an explosion of fear, tactility and perspective that the child may never have known before. Those feelings, which will become such an intrinsic part of the child's experiential map, will never feel quite as potent as they do initially, although to experience them again is what drives the child to cover new ground, heights and experiences.

Like most of the other playtypes, Exploratory Play also has its share of perceived risk attached, which each child must also learn to assess and navigate. For the child Exploratory Play is truly exploration. It is not knowing what is around the corner, or through that door, or up those stairs. If the child is not cautious, it could walk into a dog, or a group of other children, or even an oncoming vehicle. This is not good for survival. On the other hand, if the child is too cautious, it may not go anywhere, and that also bodes badly for its future. Each child must learn to navigate the planet as best it can. The play environment must not only be navigable, it must also be a place worth navigating, a place of tests, surprises and challenges, reflecting the kind of space to which a child will naturally be drawn.

To identify Exploratory Play we should look for children attempting to extend their ranging, or cautiously trying out, what are, for them, new experiences.

Fantasy and Imaginative Play

Fantasy and Imaginative Play are only different inasmuch as their subject matter is part of our reality or not. They are both mind plays and may often look the same. It is only when a child visually or verbally communicates the nature of its play that we can identify which of these two playtypes it is engaged in.

A child is engaged in Fantasy Play when components of its play narrative – a character (SpiderMan), or the setting (Topsy Turvey Land), or a power the child possesses (such as invisibility) are not drawn from the reality we experience.

Alternatively, a child is engaged in Imaginative Play when components of its play narrative – a dog, being under water, or flying an aeroplane – are drawn from reality but are clearly not external to the child's mind but a product of it.

Both playtypes may be critically important to our psychic development.

Fantasy Play, for example, provides the child's unconscious with a route through which the deeper or more 'bizarre' content of its dreams, experiences and intuitions can be given form, by becoming played-out in actions (Gregory 1987, p. 202).

Engaging in Fantasy Play both externalises material that might otherwise trouble the child, and acts to 'ground' that material in a wider, non-fantasy context. This means that the content of our unconscious, particularly that which may have been formed early in our evolution and which as children we find so disturbing in our nightmares – dragons and ghosts, for example – can be defused.

Imaginative Play provides a similar opportunity for the processing of real experiences, rather than 'evolutionary archetypes' (Stevens and Price 2000), enabling children to play-through traumatic events, and take control or alter outcomes, to enable them to achieve psychic stability and calm (Hughes 1999a).

To identify Fantasy and Imaginative Play we should look for children engaging in activity that is clearly supplemented by unseen additions. Arms outstretched and running equals flying, for example. On all fours and roaring equals a dragon; on all fours and barking equals a dog.

Locomotor Play

Locomotor Play is happening whenever children are using movement as a significant component of their play. However some games are more authentically Locomotor Play than others. Tag for example, requires locomotion for its existence. Locomotor Play is often three-dimensional, and children will use the full scope of what the play environment offers to enhance their locomotor games. Swinging can also be Locomotor Play, but only if the child is using its own locomotor effort to propel itself through the air. A child sitting passively while someone else pushes is not engaged in authentic Locomotor Play. Similarly with bikes, skates and skateboards. Only when the child is engaged in the physical act of propulsion or directional manipulation is this Locomotor Play.

Ball games, particularly unstructured versions of games like football, are also high in Locomotor Play.

A good Locomotor Play environment, that is, one with both open space and a variable landscape, will be a constant source of locomotor activity in which kickabout, running and chase games often coincide within the same space.

I once worked on an adventure playground where on Saturday afternoons a hundred children would engage in everything from football to hockey, to different chase games, basketball, dance and so on, all in the same 50m x 50m space. I remember few arguments or collisions. The children seemed very capable of navigating a dynamic, diverse and complex activity space with consummate ease. One reason for this was that no one had taken or been given ownership of the space for one single activity!

Mastery Play

Engaging in Mastery Play is how children begin to understand and develop a power relationship with the physical environment that surrounds them. That relationship is constructed from an evolving knowledge of what the environment will allow the child to do to it, and what it will not.

On the one hand, Mastery Play encapsulates the development of a physical relationship with the properties of the environment – its energy, weight, height, viscosity, flammability, strength, hardness, temperature and so on. But Mastery is also about establishing a relationship with the affective nature of spaces too. Whether it can be endured, controlled, turned into a habitat or a garden or built on. Whether it is a frightening or eerie or an elementally challenging space, like a high fell, a forest or a rugged seashore.

Engaging in Mastery Play enables children to discover and maintain a balance between their natural animal drive to dominate, and the environment's capacity to resist that domination. Above all it enables the establishment of a relationship of respect, particularly in the context of the natural, as opposed to the built environment. If such a relationship is not established early in life, then as children mature they may become foolhardy or arrogant and may underestimate the violence that the planet can unleash against them when that balance is destabilised.

Engaging in this playtype enables the development of a symbiosis between children and the world, which facilitates a learnt level of exploitation, whilst at the same time respecting the overwhelming power of the systems alongside which we all have to exist.

Developing acrobatic skills, sporting excellence and yogic flexibility are also forms of Mastery Play, but obviously they focus on mastery over one's own body. Children continually test and challenge their physical and psychic perceptions of personal endurance, to establish limits that are both satisfying and enjoyable. Like mastery of the environment, this can be taken too far, and the balance between challenge and fun can be destroyed, and may eventually just result in injury or permanent wear and tear.

Mastery Play can normally be identified whenever and wherever children are engaged in elemental forms of engagement: damming streams, holding back the tide, digging holes, creating shelters, harnessing the wind and using fire.

Object Play

Object Play is self-explanatory. From toys, to balls and puzzles, to stones, sticks, tools, and even other people, Object Play is the interaction of children with specific items in their world. The main criterion is that the object has to be an intrinsic part of the game or the focus of manipulation.

Anything that facilitates a two-way dynamic from which the child can learn, whilst at the same time learning about itself in relation to that thing, constitutes an object.

However, children will be particularly drawn to objects that appear different and interesting, and which require a flexible response from them. For example, unless a child subjects it to a geological exploration, a stone normally has only limited appeal as a play object. But a clock, or an engine, an iPod or a puzzle have much greater potential because they can be manipulated and made to do things.

It is particularly important for the playworker to be aware that all objects have potentially infinite applications as far as the child is concerned. Adults must resist the temptation to short-cut the child's discovery of the object's potential, by not only showing the child an object's use, but implying that that is both the only, and the right use for that object.

For children to gain the optimum level of flexibility of mind and body, to facilitate adaptation in a variety of contexts, it is essential that they are able to establish a creative understanding of the possibilities inherent in various components that make up their physical world.

Not only is it frustrating to be shown how to do things, if one has not asked, but it is disabling for the person on the receiving end. The great secret in facilitating Object Play is in ensuring the availability of a wide range of objects that will both attract and absorb the child. These can be almost anything, and will be dependent on the child's previous experiences, so playworkers will need to experiment.

However, be aware that Object Play can also entail playing with live objects. And whilst this manifestation of this particular play-type may be not be palatable, it does enable children to develop an understanding of their evolving relationship with the other species that inhabit the world too. Without the early engagement of this kind of Object Play, children may become permanently unempathic, cruel and exploitative in later life.

Recapitulative Play

Much has been written about this playtype since I introduced it into the revised *Playworker's Taxonomy* in 2002, and much of what has been said has been quite hostile.

In defence of its inclusion, the protocol that governs which playtypes one might include in an eventually definitive Taxonomy, currently remains fluid (Burghardt 2005), and because recapitulation is such an important idea, and because Recapitulative Play could be a very significant feature of human evolution, I think it is useful to include it here.

The idea behind recapitulation, or the Biogenetic Law, has suffered a bad press. Early advocates like Haeckel, Darwin and G. Stanley Hall, were accused of using it to supporting the eugenics movement in the early part of the twentieth century. Were those accusations true, one would understand why there is such a negative reaction to what is otherwise a fascinating idea.

I see recapitulation from a very different perspective to that of what might be called 'race ontology'. For although the original idea of recapitulation was certainly rooted in early embryological speculation, other interpretations, from which Recapitulative Play is derived and included here and in the *Playworker's Taxonomy*, offers a very different view of the idea posited in earlier works.

Rather, the work of Hall and others (Reaney 1916; Byers 1998; Burghardt 2005) leads me to conclude that recapitulation could be a vital component of the human evolutionary process and may have been so for millions of years. In other words, recapitulation is an evolutionary imperative that is rooted in natural selection, in the avoidance of extinction pressures and in our very continued existence as a species. What I draw from the work of Hall *et al.*, is that this imperative has always been most active in the play of children, irrespective of any geographical, cultural, economic or other variables that might apply.

Although he certainly wrote more about recapitulation than this, the quote from Hall (1904) that has most bearing on this discussion, is this:

the best index and guide to the stated activities of adults in past ages is found in the instinctive, untaught and non-imitative play of children.

What this says to me is 'if you look at some of what children do when they play, you will see reflected in that, some of what human beings did in the ancient past'.

At a later date, one of Hall's protégés Reaney (1916), stated that (recapitulative) play was a re-enactment of that individual's fore-bears' transmitted activities, which could be 'divided into play periods that correspond to our species "various evolutionary stages", i.e., the animal, savage, nomad, pastoral and tribal'.

What I interpret from this material is that some of what children are doing when they play might be a recap of aspects of our collective evolutionary history. It is not a specifically cultural or race recap, because children from all cultures and races manifest much the same material. Whether it is a chronological recap or simply a manifestation of 'random genetic echoes', remains to be seen.

What the idea of recapitulation and its associated play repertoires suggests, is that during our evolutionary history certain behavioural routines and mind-sets have become so important, perhaps for reasons of survival, that they became absorbed into our 'collective unconscious' (Jung 1953–1978). These have then been passed on from one generation to the next, either genetically or in some other way.

However, because these routines and mind-sets will have evolved at different times in our species evolution, i.e. at different points in the evolution of the human brain, body and consciousness, they may have been encoded differently, and a mechanism may have had to evolve to decode them and make them accessible to our internal biological processes. That is to say, material distilled and encoded – memorised – from our earliest evolutionary periods may have been physically or chemically different to that memorised from later, more recent periods.

This idea is, then, that today's children will have tens of thou-sands, if not millions of years of transmitted survival and other data stored in their bodies, in a whole variety of different forms. One assumes that the purpose of this storage process is that what is being passed on will, in some way, enable our species to survive potential extinction events similar to those in the stored memories, should they occur in the present or future. It is both the transmission and the exploration of these data through the play process that forms another key component of our neuroludic-evolutionary construct.

My question is, if survival material is passed on, and if it is in a variety of different forms, is there any evidence that a mechanism could be selected by the evolution process that would access all of this material and render it usable? There is, but it is highly tentative.

All play takes place during what is called a biologically sensitive period. 'A sensitive period in behavioural development refers to a window in development during which specific types of experience permanently alter the course of development of the brain or of other systems that support development' (Byers 1998, p. 210).

My speculation is that in much the same way as miming singing enables songbirds to rearrange and connect neural circuits and sing, during a biologically sensitive period (Kroodsma 1981), so evolution may have selected specific types of experience that I am calling Recapitulative Play, to alter the structure of inherited material and render it usable.

Thus by engaging in a particular kind of behavioural (play) routine, that incorporates the process of recapitulation, children change the nature of any transmitted/stored survival data they have inherited into a form that can be subconsciously applied to situations they may encounter in their own life.

What does Recapitulative Play look like? Perhaps the best answer is a question: 'What play routines do we see children engaging in that we might plausibly characterise as ancient or evolutionary?'

Previously (Hughes 1999b, 2001a) I have suggested the following as indicators:

- archaic/mythic and shamanistic ritual;
- fires for warmth, cooking, burning and games;

- changing identity using paints, masks and body decoration;
- large group events, like tag, wide games and other mock battles;
- den/cave building;
- all aspects of Deep Play;
- growing and preserving food;
- using weapons – bows, catapults;
- rearing other species;
- tactile sand and earth interfacing.

However, there is another facet to the notion of Recapitulative Play that has yet to be mentioned. For whilst the action of engaging in Recapitulative Play may re-arrange inherited genetic material, for reasons of survival, engaging in this process will also enable children to establish a more conscious connection with their evolutionary pasts.

Acting rather like a computer programme update, Recapitulative Play may also have been selected – I use the word advisedly – because it helps children to be more aware of the journey our species has taken to reach its current evolutionary point, emphasising how fragile is our perception of civilisation and our relationship with our habitat. In a sense this is our most critical survival lesson of all.

Although I believe there is much left to say on this topic, perhaps for the purposes of this text it is most pertinent to conclude by urging providers and facilitators of play environments to ensure that those routines that best constitute Recapitulative Play continue to be made possible and are not censored out of children's experience (Hughes 1999b).

Role Play

Role Play enables children to get a personal and a comparative fix on what is happening in the world around them, by observing and adopting both the changing old roles and the new roles that are evolving during childhood. We could be talking about parents, relatives, figures in authority like teachers, fire fighters, shopkeepers, icons like sports personalities, TV presenters, and pop stars or anyone else who appears with regularity in the children's reality.

Obviously this is not about what it is to be these people, although some children may make this mistake, out of personal need and consequent over-identification. Rather it is two things. The first is that it is a monitoring device, and in much the same way as I am suggesting Recapitulative Play acts, as an evolutionary 'playing up to speed' device. But it is also the child's interpretation of what it might be like to be these people, *within the child's frame of experience*. Role Play is helpful in enabling children to gain some understanding or an explanation of what is going on in their lives and why certain things have happened. In this sense it is a cathartic mechanism, which has the effect of empowering children in circumstances where they may feel disempowered.

However, Role Play, like the examples of several other playtypes I have used, may not convey an entirely authentic representation of what the child feels or observes. If, for example, an adult role model has power over the child, then the child's role representation of that individual may become distorted. This distorted representation is what I have termed a Stereotypical Play Narrative, or SPN (Hughes 1999a). An SPN results when the child presents back to the role model their Role Play of them: one which is mediated by the child's fear, or a similar emotion, of that model, and is adapted in some way – the intention to endear the child to the model. In other words it is a gratuitous and inaccurate representation of that particular Role Play. Children in oppressive situations may do this frequently as a survival mechanism, offering their representation of any number of models as positive distortions.

What is the impact on the child doing this representation? I suspect that the presentation of distorted representations of role models is accompanied by negative affect, like disgust or embarrassment, which the child will be unable to sustain. Eventually, the child's Role Play will disintegrate and its attempt to ingratiate itself to its oppressor will fail. This may result in a growing fear of the consequences and, further, even more distorted Role Plays will manifest as a consequence.

Role Play can be identified as an attempt at engagement in imitation of other people, through voice, mannerisms, dress and actions.

Rough and Tumble Play

This is probably the most widely researched of all the playtypes, particularly its occurrence in other species. Along with Deep Play, it is probably also the type that has suffered the highest level of prohibition, in playwork practice. Yet it has been consistently shown that there is no relationship between it and fighting, a matter about which some playworkers are fearful.

Burghardt (2005) describes Rough and Tumble Play in 'most playful species' as involving playful 'lunging, pouncing, biting, pushing, butting, grabbing, hitting, mounting and pinning' (p. 87). Whilst Baldwin (1982), describes it as 'precisely the cause of social bonding', implying that one of the functions of Rough and Tumble Play is that it enables children not only to experience a physical engagement, in which calibrating strength and agility can take place alongside more benign contacts like tickling, but that it happens with a member of the same species. This intimate, or at least, close quarter contact between children, enables them to have insights about themselves and one another, which might otherwise remain unknown.

The evidence of self-handicapping behaviour, and playful retreat by otherwise dominant play partners, strongly supports the non-aggressive evolutionary purpose of Rough and Tumble Play, suggesting instead not only a powerful calibrational, but also proto-sexual role to Rough and Tumble. Work with primates (Suomi and Harlow 1971) showed that when they were play deprived, and certainly deprived of Rough and Tumble Play, they were not only terribly disturbed, but 'when these monkeys reach physiological maturity they [were] incompetent in virtually every aspect of monkey social activity' – this was particularly the case in terms of sexual competence.

Although it may be mistaken for fighting, Rough and Tumble Play, though incorporating elements of real fighting – wrestling, chasing and so on – is friendly, physical fun, which is essential to developing an understanding of the physical 'self' in relation to rest of the physical world.

Social Play

Put simply, Social Play describes part of what happens when children playfully engage socially with other children.

As well as initially being a manifestation of the relief felt at finding other beings of similar size and outlook to oneself, the interface and interactions of Social Play gradually enable children to begin to learn the infinitely variable and basic protocol-ridden nature of human co-existence: that power and power structures exist; that one can belong or can be excluded; that one can control and manipulate and be controlled and manipulated; that one can give and receive affection and violence; that there is competition; that there is truth and lies and so on. Social Play enables children to experience these aspects of the human dynamic relatively non-detrimentally (King 1984) – meaning they can fall foul of them, make mistakes in judgement, be over confident and so on, but not be too damaged as a result.

As children interact with peers and siblings, and increasingly with adults in their play, so they also begin to realise that social interaction is very complex and fluid. Social Play relies heavily on meta-communication, on nuance, on double meanings, in-jokes, micky-taking and peer pressure. Children have to learn how to detect when someone is serious and when they are not, when someone is angry and when they are joking. They have to recognise and exist within numerous power structures that are as sophisticated and as potentially brutal as those in any 'primitive tribe' or political party. And they have to begin to learn to make rational decisions about where they stand in those complex hierarchies and understand that their actions will have consequences.

Burghardt (2005) states that Social Play contains complex features such as 'role reversal, turn taking and self-handicapping' too (p. 96).

Inevitably, Social Play has to contain argument, cruelty and repressive components. These are, and always have been, as much a part of the social dynamic as others I have mentioned. How else is power developed and exercised, for example? In this sense, like most other playtypes, Social Play has its darker side. Here, the child on the receiving end can seem toy-like, like someone being played with, and at the whim of the exponent. It can seem to the observing adult that one child is de-humanising the other, but that is rarely the case in reality (although there may be times when playworkers have to make judgement calls about this).

As with the other playtypes, each child is exploring the interface between them. None of them has any conscious advantage or special knowledge, as adults may infer. They can only use what they have and use the skills and insights they have learnt. As children from physically 'tough' homes will employ what they have experienced in their Social Play, so children from intellectual, religious, wealthy, musical, or creative homes will employ what they too have learnt. That some children use language, or actions or techniques or skills that others do not, is simply a reflection of the diversity we all have to learn to navigate.

Social Play is a visible manifestation of the diversity of experience and drives of our species. Needless to say, there will be certain forms of social interaction between children that some adults may want discouraged: sexual, violent and risky interactions, for example.

Burghardt (2005) recognised this, stating that 'play may be prox-imally controlled by a broad array of emotions, not just fun'. He also cites Sutton-Smith who suggests that much play in humans may be a means of triggering 'virtual emotions' in safe contexts (p. 140) – meaning that as their 'emotional intelligence' (Payne 1985) is evolv-ing, so children experiment with aspects of their being that are emotionally charged: aspects such as sex and sexuality, for example. This may manifest itself on a play project, either as proto-sexual behaviour, where children in middle-childhood (7–10) begin to relate to other children as sexual beings, in conversation, meta-communication and in physical contacts like play fighting and hand holding, or between older children, as more overt sexual experimentation.

To identify Social Play look for any well-established (or even less well-established) adult behavioural traits as they are played through children.

Socio-Dramatic Play

Socio-Dramatic Play is the mechanism evolution has selected to enable the exorcism of 'difficult' social and emotional situations in children's lives. Using the construction of dramatic social 'scenes' children can 'play through' situations they may have experienced as painful, embarrassing or frightening, at school, at home or elsewhere. These situations can be negotiated in the relative emotional safety of the play situation. It could be something as traumatic as being hit, or witnessing domestic violence, or parents arguing, or bereavement, to something as benign as watching a 'scary' episode of a TV programme, or falling out with a friend.

In Hughes (1999a), I cited an extreme example of Socio-Dramatic Play, describing an imagined scenario of a child overhearing an adult discussing both murdering someone and the circumstances surrounding the actual act. I explored how the child, fearful of what it had heard, might engage in a form of reconstruction of the event, where it was able to redistribute power or control, so that it was able to resolve the event in its imagination in a form that was no longer experienced as fearful.

Although perhaps more frequently observed in therapeutic sessions, instances of Socio-Dramatic Play are not uncommon on some play spaces. For example, they may take place where children are able to build dens and set up social situations, or where there is comparatively secluded space where children can re-enact and reconstruct what they experience as acutely private or intimate situations, without being overlooked by adults or other children not a part of the play.

Like the successful emergence of all the other playtypes, Socio-Dramatic Play relies on a non-judgemental play environment ambiance. As it is impossible successfully to imagine being a horse, if other children laugh at you when you try, so it is difficult to play through a difficult domestic scene if it becomes an entertainment for other children.

The main difference between Dramatic and Socio-Dramatic play is that in the latter the situations are drawn from the child's day-to-day 'reality' and are either still happening or have happened recently. Socio-Dramatic Play is an important safety valve for children in highly-charged social situations, where they might be experiencing difficulties from bullying teachers or from other children at school, or having to live with the difficulty of surviving a home life with parents or siblings who are abusive, drunk, drugged or mentally ill (Hughes 1988, 2001a).

Episodes of Socio-Dramatic Play can be recognised by their 'real-life' contexts, their high emotional charge and the realisation that, for all of their visible congruence, what is often being played out is far from what most of us would describe as being normal.

Symbolic Play

Although 'symbolism' is the representation of the non-material, Symbolic Play can take many forms, which whilst sometimes expressing what is abstract, may also express what is not there, or that of which the child has no experience.

Whilst some children may be able to symbolise abstract notions like 'country' or 'loyalty' with flags and colours, others will use a rope to define a patch of shark-infested water, wooden bricks to represent a 'magic' tower, a circle to represent the sun, or a squiggle to represent 'where I live'.

Different episodes of Symbolic Play can map the emergence of a developing ability to visualise life's abstract as well as its material components. For example, a drawing a child makes this year could be a representation of the sun, whereas next year, a similar shape could be used to represent a 'holiday', which for many children would be a more abstract concept. One year, a squiggle could represent 'where I live', whilst next year it could represent 'happiness', again a more abstract idea.

It is a struggle for most adults to express abstractions, so they resort to any means available – particularly the visual (writing, maths, maps, paintings) and the auditory (music, poetry), in an attempt to convey what they are feeling, sensing, intuiting and dreaming. So it is no surprise that children do the same.

Adults have always used symbolic representations to help them to 'see' the invisible. 'Heat and wind activate their symbolic indices, the thermometer and weathervane,' says Quine (Gregory 1987, p. 764).

Why we choose what we choose to symbolise what we want to symbolise, implies that 'fanciful subconscious resemblances must be assumed between symbol and symbolised' (Gregory, ibid., p. 674). Wilber (1996) takes this further, suggesting that the magical world of symbolic thinking was 'conscious in our remote ancestors' (ibid. p. 54). Could this mean that what we choose to use as symbols may have been internalised by our ancestors and recapitulated through a combination of Recapitulative and Symbolic Play?

In a passage that echoes the early development of the mind and may parallel children's symbolic thinking in early childhood, Quine also describes the world as 'plastic and shaped at whim, [where] condensation and displacement rule, [and] wholes and parts become each other' (Gregory, 1987, p. 764) – demonstrating succinctly how apparently confused may be the child's early attempts at symbolising the material and non-material.

This overlapping world of dreams and 'reality', what Neumann (1973) described as 'this primitive magical state', that our ancestors lived, and which 'still lives on in us', may be what children experience as they attempt to put meaning to emotion and ideas.

However, this state, although 'still alive in us today', seems to have been compressed into two main areas of psychic activity – childhood and dreams. Freud is quoted as saying, 'What once dominated waking life, while the mind was still young and incompetent, seems now to have been banished into the night' (Wilber 1996, p. 54).

Here again is the connection between Symbolic and Recapitulative Play. Is it plausible that we retain more than just the *capacity* to move into this magic state? That as recapitulation may bring into contemporary play patterns, experiences passed on, perhaps from the dawn of time, so Symbolic Play may enable children to access distant reaches of the human psyche and utilise what they find there, enabling them to make sense of life today?

Symbolic Play can be identified as children attempting to engage in any medium that makes possible the representation of an abstract, emotional or dreamlike idea or concept: for one child, it was an arrangement of lolly sticks in the dirt that made a pattern, for another it was a noise that represented her feelings for a particular film star.

On one playground where I worked, we flew a huge 4m x 3m flag on the top of one of the playground's towers. There was one word on the flag – FREEDOM. At the time, the flag crackling in the wind was intended to symbolise what the playground stood for – a space in which children could immerse themselves in their own agenda – free from the pressures of home, school and system (Hughes 2001a).

Chapter Four

The realisation that play is a generic term that can be broken down into a number of very different components called playtypes that as Burghardt (1998) wrote, 'may have different causal bases, functions, phylogenies and ontogenies', is probably quite alarming for anyone labouring under the misconception that play is one thing; a perspective that falls within the limits of their own behavioural and moral preconceptions.

For the playworker this same realisation, although daunting, can also be liberating. For one thing, the advent of playtypes makes playwork sixteen times more complicated and therefore sixteen times more interesting. Needless to say, it also makes it sixteen times more demanding!

Identifying, understanding and providing for the different playtypes also has the effect of changing playwork significantly, moving it away from its traditional roots, of a 'one size fits all' play environment construct, into one in which terms like complexity, comprehensiveness, compensation and deprivation, come more into the fore.

This chapter explores what these terms mean in a playwork context and discusses how playwork practice may need to evolve to address them.

PlayTypes and Playwork Practice

Complexity
The doorway to exploring play as a set of interlocking routines that are the outward manifestation of complex evolutionary currents.

As the last chapter demonstrates, not only are playtypes the names we give to what we see children doing – singing, climbing, digging, pretending and ranging, for example, they also describe external representations of the evolution process, as it displays itself through the vehicle of the child's play.

What might the implications of this development be for playwork practice?

Playtypes and neural development
With the growing body of evidence that play stimulates brain growth during a specific 'sensitive period' (Huttenlocher 1990, 1992; Kotulak 1996) and that it also has a significant role in the creation of adaptive flexibility (Bruner 1972; Sylva 1977; Burghardt 1998), play-work practice is already having to recognise and adapt to a new analysis of its responsibilities.

However, at least from a theoretical playwork perspective, another question relating to the role of play in brain development also needs some consideration. If play in a generic sense stimulates brain growth, might individual playtypes stimulate the growth of specific areas of the brain? In other words, do different playtypes have the growth of specific areas of the brain 'allocated' to them?

Already, the research suggests a relationship between the physical act of playing and the anatomical construction or placement of neural tissue. It is not a huge theoretical leap then, to suggest that by engaging in different physical acts, i.e. in different playtypes, neural tissue may be constructed or placed in locations specified by engaging that specific playtype.

In fact, given that

play may be a means of consolidating not just specific behavioural routines, like predation or reproduction, but of enabling the formation of the neural foundations, known as substrates, necessary for complex negotiation in a three dimensional world. (Burghardt 1998)

and that the mechanism for creating a flexible brain may be

the production of an over abundance of cells and synapses, which the brain has to use to make itself work (Sutton-Smith 1997, citing Gould 1996, p. 223)

then the role of different playtypes, may be to lay early specific neural foundations in children, which do not in themselves create behaviour, but which actually enable behaviour and cognition to be created. (Hughes 1999a, 2001a).

Imagine this, for a moment. At birth, there exists in the child a circular feedback mechanism that connects the child's brain to the environment via a gradually more complicating process of playing. The embryonic brain, which already contains otherwise redundant cells, created by 'play fragments', reaches out to the environment using arms and legs to make its contact. Having been contacted, the environment conveys a basic sensory message regarding its nature

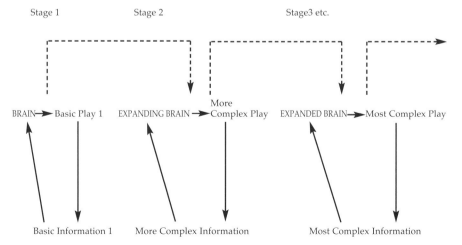

to the child's brain, which responds by integrating that information, and reaching out to make a more complicated playful exploration of the environment. What this next exploration yields is a more complex picture of that environment: a picture which is then integrated into the child's brain, using those otherwise redundant neurones.

What this suggests is the existence of a fundamental relationship between play and brain construction, that is between brain construction and play construction: that whilst the child may be born with the basic paradigms of each playtype within cells, or genes, each playtype and the brain retain a high enough level of flexibility to adapt to the environment in which they are born.

Now how the brain might do this, although an interesting question, is not really the province of either pure or applied playwork, but the possibility that playtypes may themselves evolve differently with different kinds of experience, is an interesting thought. If that is the case, then the way playtypes evolve in the children with whom we work tells us something about how the brain and play collude in different environments and sheds light on the adaptive and perhaps the evolutionary processes themselves, particularly when a comparative analysis of the relationship between play and environment becomes possible.

Currently, all of this is wildly speculative and deeply theoretical. But it does demonstrate that playwork could benefit from more knowledge in three specific areas of playtype manifestation. The first is: What in any play routine, is the precursor to the onset of a particular playtype? The second is: Can that playtype be broken down into any predictable components or sub-routines? The third is: How does a particular playtype decay once it has been manifested?

Clearly, as playwork roots itself further in evolutionary and other ideas, our understanding will become more comprehensive, and that will impact on our practice. The external look of the playspace may change little, but the systems that operate it cannot avoid becoming increasingly sophisticated.

Comprehensiveness
Ensuring that the play opportunities on offer reflect all playtypes.

Currently playwork acknowledges sixteen playtypes as the total of sub-sets that constitute play. The major practical challenge presented by this is how to ensure that children have access to the props, ambiance and other environmental and psychological resources that may be essential to manifesting each distinct play-type. For example:

Space
One obvious prerequisite is space. Perhaps because, at present, most people's perception of play is that it is a single phenomenon, play environments tend to be far too small to facilitate the manifestation of all sixteen playtypes. Play spaces in the future will need to be significantly larger than most of them currently are.

Permissions
Another is 'permissions' (Melville 1996). Provided by auditory or visual cues, adult actions and 'free' activity, permissions ensure that children 'know' when a space is 'a play space', and that whatever play is, it can be done there.

Capacity and potential for different frames
The playspace must have the 'capacity' and 'potential' for children to create the frames (Else and Sturrock 1998), within which each of the playtypes can be manifested.

Capacity means that the playspace contains the realistic possibility that each of the playtypes can be manifested by a number of children, simultaneously. It is less about space in a general sense, than it is about the types of spaces that are available (see Hughes 1996b for more).

Potential refers to what is in each of these spaces, which will enhance and enrich the experience for the child. On previous occasions I have referred to props (Hughes 2001a, 2001b). The presence of props increases the potential of a space to facilitate a comprehensive range of playtypes.

Resisting censorship

All too often playworkers bow to inappropriate pressure from the children's parents and carers, or even from their own employers, which suggests that engaging in a particular playtype should not be permitted for all kinds of spurious reasons: bullying, sexual contact, getting messy, political incorrectness, danger of getting hurt, and so forth.

Of course, thought should be given to children's capabilities when they are engaging in a particular playtype in a particular context, and no playworker should put a child at anything other than transitional physical or psychological risk. That means that the risk is there, it is real, but it is also being monitored. This does affect the nature of the experience of course. If a child was playing in the wild, without supervision s/he would have to deal with different risks without any safety net other than his/her own judgement, which normally provides a sufficient safeguard. On the playground, there has to be a safety net of sorts, in recognition of the artificial nature of the space. However, it is still important that what risks are present, are as real and as comprehensible as possible, or important survival lessons may not be learnt.

Thus as far as is possible, all *playtypes should be permitted, even if that means that some may be tamer than they would be in the wild.*

Environmental modification

Because playwork is about providing *opportunities* for experiences, rather than about ensuring that those experiences are accessed, we can ethically provide for each playtype, safe in the knowledge that the worst that will happen is that children will be able to access experiences that otherwise they would not. At best what will happen is that (whilst knowledge of the neurological benefits of play is still sketchy) homogeneous, comprehensive, neural stimulation is available to children.

But we can see from this statement alone that playwork is an incredibly precarious ethical tightrope on which to have to balance. We want children to be in total control, yet we also want to ensure that what should be in their play environment, from the perspective of 'free ranging and the quest for enrichment', is also there. We must not make the space too neophilic, i.e. novel, or we will be manipulating the play drive. But the playspace must be neophilic enough or children may not realise that certain features are there at all and not use them.

This brings me to the question: is playwork attempting to produce a particular kind of child? The answer is, no, it is not. However, what it is trying to ensure is that each child, irrespective of background, disability, culture, is able, should it feel so impelled, to access a graduated set of foundational biological experience we call play experiences. To ensure that they are as physically and psychologically prepared, as good play experiences can make them, to face their own future on the planet.

Play policy

Many children are disadvantaged and have very limited play opportunities or impoverished play experiences. These children are also spread right across the socio-economic spectrum. For the poor, there is no choice unless central governments develop a National Play Policy to address the play and environmental deficits these children face. For the better-off there are playful choices, but many parents still opt for non-playful tuition or for after-school and weekend 'activities' that are not, in themselves, playful. It is no surprise that many children who experience this 'fast-track' childhood become 'adult' before their time and see the world through a quasi-adult prism, incapable of either relating to other children, or to their own natural drive to play.

It is only with the advent of the political will to develop play policies through the political process, that access to the full range of playtypes – as of right, to all children – will be guaranteed.

As I write, Wales is the only country in the world, as far as I am aware, that has what I would call a genuine play policy, and even in the Welsh Play Policy, access to *all* playtypes is not mentioned. The Republic of Ireland has also attempted the development of a play policy for its children, although a totally play-driven policy, may be some time away. Northern Ireland is also moving towards the development of a play policy too, and given what children there have had to endure in the recent past, this is also a very hopeful sign.

However, the question is when will the larger populations begin to take this important step? England currently lags behind, although this is changing as I write, and, notwithstanding the Scandinavian social pedagogue developments, very little is happening either in Europe, Asia or the US.

Recently, I wrote that any play policy must now satisfy what I called bio-evolutionary criteria, like facilitating each of the known playtypes, rather than the socio-cultural criteria that have informed policy development up to the present time. In the same piece I also said that I was concerned that we seem unable to distinguish between the two, let alone accommodate the former. As the vital relationship between play and evolution becomes more evident it becomes ever more crucial that our priorities for our young increasingly recognise their need to play (Hughes 2005).

This is the challenge of the next decade for any number of countries. The development of policies that recognise the present and future danger we are in, with respect to our need to play as a species and the fact that children are playing less and less, are as important, if not more so, than policies relating to global warming, energy conservation, arms proliferation and so on. With play-based policies in place, children everywhere will have the chance to re-evaluate their planet and the place of our species on it. Without them, forms of extinction beckon.

Compensation

To compensate for a range of playtype deficits children may be experiencing. As a design template when developing a playspace or modifying an existing feature.

In order that they can access the play experiences they need, children first have to locate those play experiences. They do this first by ranging, so that they can encounter different play possibilities, and then by experimenting with the new environments they discover on their travels. However, many contemporary children either do not, or cannot range. Traffic, in particular, is a serious modern problem in this context. It is just too dangerous for young children to attempt to cross busy roads in order to discover new ludic landscapes.

Many play habitats used by generations of children also keep disappearing. Housing and industry bury them under concrete or poison them with pollution, roads are driven through them and the construction of golf courses and other leisure facilities claim them for adult use.

However, the most insidious problem of current times is probably fear. Parents are terrified to let their children range for fear of abduction and worse. And children seem increasingly reluctant to range for fear of bullies.

What this means is that many children are not playing in any liberated, empowering sense. Instead they are left to try to acquire a comprehensive play experience in their back yard, in bedrooms or close to where they live. Recent research (Huttenmoser and Degan-Zimmermann 1995) demonstrates that this is less than appropriate.

Children cannot get the comprehensive experience they need in such experientially restricted situations. Instead they need to range to discover the levels and diversity of experience that will challenge them, and help them to grow in knowledge and in complexity of response, becoming increasingly confident.

What practical playwork does to address this, is provide diverse and challenging environments in which children can play, without ranging. This cannot replace the quality of ranging, exploration and discovery that unfettered play gives children, but it can go a long way towards compensating for their loss and its accompanying disability.

However, with the provision of environments for children's play, whether they are adventure playgrounds, after school clubs, summer playschemes, or whatever, come serious responsibilities. Play has a significant evolutionary role (Burghardt 2005), and to be deprived of it can lead to horrendous problems for the children affected, as we will see in the next section.

Therefore, if we are going to make provision that is intended to compensate for the loss or unavailability of certain play experiences in children's lives, we need to be sure that that is what we are actually doing.

If we assume that children regularly seek to experience all sixteen playtypes, but that the opportunities to experience a number of them may not be there – it may, for example, be impossible for them to dress up (recapitulation), to dig or light fires (mastery), meet other children (social), make flags (symbolic), or play off-ground touch (locomotor) – then our practical playwork response should be that we design the provision we make to compensate for those missing experiences/playtypes.

What this means, is that we need to be able to assess the child's local play environment, for the playtype opportunities it holds, and then provide for the ones it does not. (See Hughes 2001a, pp. 91–6 and Hughes 2001b, p. 31, for assessment scheme examples.)

However, diversity does not mean providing just one experience to address each playtype. When children range, they are attracted to enriched habitats that might contain say six different experiences for engaging in each playtype – perhaps more. The challenge for playwork practice is to ensure that the experiences children have as a consequence of the playwork input, are as authentic to natural, adult-free, evolution-guided experience, as children would encounter in a natural, diverse and unadaulterated space.

A major problem with 'supervised' provision, for the playing child, is that s/he is made constantly aware that the provision is contrived or artificial. In 'real' play, children are and always have been, in control of what they do and of why they do it. It is almost certainly this, plus the content of the environment, that is so potent for evolutionary purposes. The organism – the child – intuits what to play with that will provide the greatest benefit.

In supervised play provision, this is sometimes not understood, and so there is a constant struggle between child and playworker for control of the experience. This is even further confused by the additional imposition of spurious equality and other agendas, which would not see the light of day in a child-controlled space. This does not mean that children have no notion of justice, equality and fairness; rather that they operate these ideas differently to adults. Adults may have one way of applying them, whereas children, as with everything else they do, try out any number of approaches, some of which may not be to the adult's taste, but are perfectly valid nonetheless.

Thus, if a major part of playwork practice is to compensate for any deficit in playtypes experience children may encounter, appropriateness of response is perhaps the qualitative bottom line. Playworkers must take great care to avoid their intervention becoming an opportunity for them as individuals, or for their organisations or authorities, to adulterate the play experience for children, or they will simply be engaged in a domestication or citizenship exercise, rather than one that facilitates quality, evolutionary play experiences.

Deprivation
Addressing play deprivation.

Increasingly, the playwork practitioner is having to consider the probability of having to provide play opportunities for children whose playtypes experience to date has either been distorted or significantly deprived. And who, because of the impact of these abnormal experiences, are showing symptoms ranging from unhappiness to florid psychosis.

How s/he might do this is almost a clinical question and outside the bounds of playwork, but it might be helpful to start there, nonetheless.

All over the world, medical professionals have a construct of what constitutes a healthy human being. They also have a perception of the symptoms that occur when human beings become unhealthy, and a perception of the conditions necessary to maintain health. Using this information, they have devised a diagnostic procedure.

Stevens and Price (2000, p. 5) describe it thus. They

- recognise specific symptoms;
- define the syndrome;
- identify the tissue pathology;
- demonstrate the causes of the tissue pathology;
- establish an appropriate cure.

However, if the symptoms can be avoided in the first place, by focusing on the factors that cause the illness and its accompanying symptoms, using a preventative strategy, so much the better.

Look at malnutrition for example:

Question	Answer
What is the illness/state?	Malnutrition
What are its symptoms?	Weight loss
What are the causes of the illness/state?	Inadequate nourishment
Can the causes be addressed prior to the onset of the illness/state?	Yes
What strategy should be instituted?	Appropriate feeding regime
What would indicate success?	Weight gain

Playwork and prevention

As yet playwork has neither the knowledge base nor the resources to offer the reality of a sophisticated diagnostic sequence like the one outlined by Stevens and Price, but even so, it can offer a simple preventative strategy similar to that offered for malnutrition.

By taking as our starting point the primary studies on play deprivation (for example Brown and Lomax 1969; Hughes 1988; Huttenmoser and Degan-Zimmerman 1995; Chugani 1996, 1998; Brown 1998) we can construct a similar model:

Question	Answer
What is the illness/state?	Playtypes deprivation
What are its symptoms?	A continuum from unhappiness to aggression to PTDP[*]
What are the causes of the illness/state?	Inadequate or inappropriate access to playtypes
Can the causes be addressed prior to the onset of the illness/state?	Yes
What strategy should be instituted?	Ensure regular access to diverse interpretations of all playtypes
What would indicate success?	Happy/balanced children

[*]PTDP = PlayTypes Deprivation Psychosis. It is this term, rather than Play Deprivation Psychosis or PDP, that I am going to use here to describe the lethally violent behaviour in those cases, supposedly affected by chronic play deprivation, as cited in Brown 1998.

However, although this gives us a comparative preventative strategy, we still need more information to make a rudimentary diagnosis. Malnutrition is the result of chronic malnourishment, but what might be the result of PlayTypes Deprivation Psychosis or its precursors of unhappiness?

What is Playtypes Deprivation Psychosis and what causes it?

As there is an established relationship between play and physical/psychological health (Huttenmoser and Degan-Zimmerman 1995; Brown 1998; Siviy 1998, amongst others) we can assert that a ludically healthy child will be one who regularly engages in each of the basic playtypes. By implication, a child who does not regularly engage in each of the basic playtypes will be ludically unhealthy to a greater or lesser extent, and will show symptoms as a consequence.

Children's ludic health

With this in mind then, one of the playworker's primary functions is to ensure that within the boundaries of the space s/he constructs and operates, the opportunity to engage in each playtype, on a scale commensurate with the child's abilities, is available to each of those who use that space. This guarantees that every child who chooses regularly to engage (and there will be those who do not) with the whole range of playtypes will be able to do so and will be happy and balanced as a consequence. However, this is still a theoretical proposition and will only be proved one way or the other by further observational research.

Play, evolutionary anticipation and play deprivation

There are good theoretical reasons for suggesting that children who do not engage comprehensively with all playtypes might show a range of symptoms as a consequence. Hughes (2005) begins to outline why.

> I visualise playing as two interconnected processes. First; as the builder of sensory bonds between the child and the external world and second; as a conduit for an increasingly complex information flow from the environment to the child and from the child to the environment. An information flow that has an impact both on the (essential) generation of neural and muscular tissue in the child (Burghardt 1998), and on the child's ability to identify, access and understand new and more advanced information. (See also Sutton-Smith 1997, quoting Kotulak 1996, p. 223.)

I contend that for this process to occur at all in children generally, it needs to be *anticipated* in some way, by the genetic and embryonic mechanisms within the child: i.e. that for millions of years, the human body has been gradually modified by evolution to engage in play for these reasons.

And, if this process is anticipated, that is expected by the child's internal drives as the child grows, that there are consequential processes that either do not happen or that happen at a far from optimum level if children do not engage in all playtypes. Evolutionary anticipation forms another vital plank in our evolving neuroludic-evolutionary construct.

Panic, distress and crisis

For example, the child would initially experience panic and distress. If a child suffocates through a lack of anticipated oxygen, or starves through a lack of anticipated nutrition, or misses the love and attachment it anticipates from its primary carer, panic and distress would be its initial reaction. And this reaction would escalate if the deficit were prolonged as demonstrated by a baby's heart-rending separation call, the most primitive and basic mammalian vocalisation (MacLean 1985; Balbernie 2001).

In other words, if play is the evolved mechanism for incredibly important biological processes such as

- adaptation and flexibility (Bruner 1972; Lorenz 1972; Sylva 1977);
- brain and muscle growth (Beckoff and Byers 1998; Burghardt 1998);
- conscious thought (Damasio 1994; Brown 1998);

and if the child does not play or only plays in a distorted manner, then it will experience something similar to what Grof (1975), termed an 'agonising existential crisis', as millions of years of unsatisfied anticipation come crashing down around it. I imagine that this terrible sub-conscious realisation of an apparent disconnectedness between the evolutionary process and the child may act as the precursor to the PlayTypes Deprivation Psychosis, referred to above.

Causes and effects

In short, play deprivation inhibits the anticipated evolutionary connection between the child, its evolutionary past (as described in Hall's Recapitulation Theory) and everything else around it. This lack of connectedness creates the kind of dehumanised state, which at low intensities brings about symptoms of unhappiness, and which, at higher intensities, develops the capacity to murder people in cold blood.

Brown and Lomax (1969) studied the case of a student who had killed seventeen people. They reported that,

> His violent acts [were] triggered by his sense of powerlessness, humiliation and entrapment [brought about by] his inability to find coping techniques through play, humour, self reciprocal friendships and other distancing and stress lowering habits. (Brown 1998, p. 248)

Another way of putting this, is that the student was being overwhelmed by events against which he had been unable to develop any defences or alternative interpretations through play during his childhood.

I have proposed above that playing is the mechanism whereby human children make contact with the world and with the past, and learn how to navigate what they encounter. So if children do not play, they do not make the necessary contacts. If they do not make the necessary contacts, then they do not develop the ability to navigate.

One effect of any failure of play to be activated, is that the secretion of extreme levels of neurochemicals may be triggered, which in their turn may create extremes of mood that result in violent behaviour (Zuckerman 1969, 1984). In other words, the potential neurochemical equilibrium that would register as normality for that individual could be seriously disturbed by play deprivation, and may in some cases even reach those levels that result in a tendency towards lethally violent behaviour.

Psychic disintegration

As in its extreme form, play deprivation means being detached from the most fundamental sensory and emotional connections both with the planet and with everything on it, I find myself continually drawn to referring to its effects as 'psychic disintegration' (Ogden 2001, pp. 92–104).

Playing develops a graduated interface between the child and the universe that enables exploration and assimilation to take place and evolve, so that at each stage of its development – because the form that this exploration and assimilation are taking is commensurate with the child's developmental perceptions -the child is 'at ease' with its view and interpretation of its existence.

If the child is deprived of play for whatever reason, its unconscious capacity to create this balance – a balance that is essential to its mental well-being – is diminished, and perhaps destroyed. The consequence is that the child is left suspended in a sensory and psychic void that provides it with no reliable reference with which to make physical or psychic connections and interpret its life. Existence literally becomes meaningless.

It is this 'disintegration' of the child's evolving capacity for psychic evaluation, coupled with the physical demands of reality, that create the lethal cocktail of toxic neurochemical levels, which may result in 'PlayTypes Deprivation Psychosis' and the random and pointless violence, cited in Brown 1998.

The child must choose

For children in a whole variety of circumstances, from bleak living environments to abusive family situations, a degree of PDP is a potential consequence, simply because these situations deprive children of experiences that indicate the spectrum of diversity, essential to good mental health.

However, from a practical viewpoint, it is essential that the playworker does not over-react and force children to play, because of the possibility of developing PDP if they do not. I am convinced that the potency/efficacy of play to deliver its biologically essential outcomes, resides in the child's control over its reaction to its drive to play. In other words, the more we (playworkers or adults in general) intervene in children's actual play experiences, the less biologically effective the experience will be for the child.

Koestler, quoted in Vandenberg 1978 said as much, when he stated: 'The more contaminated something is with other motives, the less it is play.'

If children are to be able to exercise control over what they do in the environments playworkers create and operate, playworkers have to come to terms with their long-held ethical stance that play belongs to the child, and that whether or not to play, or to play comprehensively is, in the end, the child's choice. Playworkers can make comprehensive provision and they can make that provision accessible and interesting, but then they have to leave the decision to engage or not, to the child. If they do not, they adulterate the experience and replace a complex biological process that has taken many years to evolve, simply out of short-term expediency.

So if a child chooses a narrow engagement, or if her or his friends choose a narrow engagement, this should be respected. But given what has been said above, attempts should also be made to make other playtypes easily accessible and interesting as a way of over-riding children's prejudices against them: for example linking football to art in some way, or computer games to locomotor activity.

However, this is about positioning and fine-tuning, and not about advocating that playworkers actively encourage children to engage in other, or new activities. To do that would undermine the child's own intrinsic motivation and immerse playwork in the ethical quag-mire alluded to above.

Diversity is all

It might appear from what has been written, that football or computer games do not implicitly contain or subsume each or most of our currently identified playtypes, and that is not true. Both computer games and football are extraordinarily complex phenomena whose components might easily include aspects of the majority of playtypes.

Having said that however, playing computer games does not usually include engaging in 3D locomotor activity, for example, and whilst football, like other sports, is an incredibly enriched activity, engaging in it can be rather exclusive and obsessive. Children who engage in it often do so to the exclusion of other things and, as a result, may experience a level of playtypes deprivation. This logic also applies to other activities that dominate some children's lives.

However, playworkers must be careful not to be guilty of offloading their own prejudices or preconceptions onto the children with whom they work. Perhaps they should also be asking: Might children benefit from engaging with hobbies, interests, fashions and crazes that are different from their preferred choices? What does the term 'rounded individual' mean? What is wrong with building one's life around an activity like football if it makes one happy?

The playwork response has to be predicated on the notion of the 'quality' of the experience one has, and how it facilitates adaptation. Sutton-Smith (1997) suggests that a part of play's function is to keep neural material flexible to change, avoiding what he calls 'rigidification' of behaviour:

> Biologically, its [play's] function is to reinforce the organism's variability in the face of rigidifications of successful adaptation (as formulated by Gould). This variability covers the full range of behaviour from the actual to the possible. (p. 231)

Playful variability has many facets. For example, Sylva (1977) states, 'Natural selection would favour the most playful individuals ... for they have acquired more useful information about the potential of the environment and their actions on it" (p. 60). So from that perspective, playing football is certainly not a bad thing, in fact it is probably a very good thing. But because life itself, and the environs in which it unfolds, are so diverse, children need many different experiences to those provided solely by doing any one thing, if the benefits they get from playing are going to significantly support their survival and their sanity in a whole variety of different locations and circumstances.

PlayTypes as meta-communication

In the same paper, Sylva cites Loizos (1967), Eibl-Eibesfeldt (1967, 1970) and Bruner (1972, 1974) as claiming that the essence of play lies in 'combinatorial flexibility, where the playing [child] borrows bits of behaviour from survival patterns ... [and then] ... string[s] these bits of behaviour together to form novel solutions to problems requiring the re-structuring of thought or action' (p. 60).

At the heart of combinatorial flexibility is diversity of experience, because it is this that acts as the engine for the supply of the 'bits' to 'borrow'. At the heart of this diversity of experience, is regular engagement in each of the playtypes.

As each child develops, it manifests each playtype in a range of 'forms', as a means of engaging with the world in new ways and on new levels. However, the actual 'form' each of the playtypes takes at any given time, as well as being dictated by the child's own physical and psychological capabilities, is dictated by the nature of the experience the child is driven to by its emotional 'state'.

So, to the usual forms of meta-communication that children evolve and use so profoundly, we can add the numerous 'forms' of playtypes, which, like facial expressions and body postures, also act to convey the intricacies of a child's 'state' to those around them, especially other children. This information can then be responded to by them, perhaps as a part of a playful engagement. More of this later.

PlayTypes and the playworker

I want to finish this chapter with just a few words on the inevitable effects of playtypes theorising on playworkers themselves. Although I have alluded to this before (Hughes 2001b), as the analysis becomes deeper, so the potential impact on the playworker may also increase.

What started off as a relatively short and simple journey to explore some basic perceptions of sixteen different ways of playing, has deepened within these pages into a marathon of playwork theory, which draws from sources neurological and metaphysical, as well as experiential.

I anticipate playworkers asking: why does it have to be so complicated? My response is that simplicity does not necessarily lead to accuracy. The only way to ensure accuracy, or a more correct, informed discourse is to follow this marathon to its natural conclusion: a conclusion which I anticipate will itself be a form of simplicity, but one we can trust to ensure an appropriate qualitative response to the situation in which children today find themselves. That is, needing to play, but often unable to do so.

I feel particularly concerned for the faceworker, who is battling to ensure that provision continues to be funded and staffed. Of what possible use can this exploration of playtypes be to her or him?

I have often likened playwork to astronomy. Astronomy is a discipline that explores and studies the stars and, as that exploration has proceeded, so the incredible has been superseded by the awesome, as astronomers have evolved new telescopes and other instruments and, as a consequence, have discovered new stars, black holes and anti-matter. In other words, no one could have contemplated, or even imagined, what research into the universe would have discovered.

I feel much the same about playwork. Making sure children continue to be able to play in as free and natural a manner as is possible, is, we think, very important for our children's happiness, and their physical and psychological health and well-being. Observing our children as they play, is perhaps as important to our species as adults, as playing is to them as children.

Already, work on playtypes is beginning to throw up fascinating questions about what it is we are observing, but in reality we have hardly started clarifying the awesome nature of both the children we seek to serve and their play.

Everything children do seeks to convey something to the world outside their entities. Do we yet understand that language; do we yet speak it? Or, more like scientists in the Middle Ages, are we looking up into the sky towards the stars and concluding they are silent and dead, simply because we have yet to invent the equivalent of a radio telescope, a device that will transform these 'silent heavenly bodies' into babbling communicators?

All that is happening to good playwork practice as we theorise and perhaps as a result, understand more, is better fine-tuning: recognising a need to check that certain props are available on a daily basis; ensuring that all playtypes are available to children; reminding ourselves that the ambiance of the playspace allows *play* to happen, as a priority over macho-sports, or TV soap operas.

Children who have access to good provision are, in my opinion, the lucky ones. Now our challenge is to find ways of working with those who to date, do not enjoy such access.

Our greatest challenge, after making good provision for all children, is in improving our understanding of the relationship between playing and fighting off those pressures of extinction that threaten us continually, as a species. Scientists have long asserted that play is incredibly important to our survival as a species. These days they seem even more confident in this assertion. If they are correct, and I believe they are, then it would be odd indeed, if whilst we were making provision for play, engaged in environmental modification of playspaces, observing and interpreting playtypes routines, exploring quality and so on, that we did not do what we can at the same time to inform others of what our senses and intuitions are 'picking-up' on the playground, in playcentres and so on.

Only recently, a colleague told me of a concern he had: that until recently his perception was that playworkers, whatever else their differences, shared a common play culture of fires, dens and magic places, as examples. But now, he said, he was meeting prospective playworkers with no concept of play as he understood it.

Is it possible that we are now encountering a generation of potentially play-deprived playworkers? Has a new playtype mutated? Are dens and fires redundant as playtypes foci? I do not know.

What I do know, is that children, their opportunity to play and the quality and relevance of their play provision, will all benefit from this kind of questioning and theorising. Hopefully so will the rest of us.

The final three chapters take us further on this theoretical journey: exploring playtypes in even more detail, and demonstrating their theoretical complexity.

PART II

Chapter Five

We have now had a closer look at each of the sixteen playtypes presented in the Playworker's Taxonomy *and explored how a clearer identification and understanding of them can help us to both comprehend play's complexity and why we need to make provision that addresses comprehensiveness, compensation and deprivation.*

However, this only covers a part of what is playtypes' potential; for playtypes may also have different developmental stages as well as a whole variety of slightly different manifestations.

In this chapter, 'Types of PlayTypes', we briefly explore these different aspects of the sixteen playtypes, that we will now call 'Basic', or 'Singular' playtypes and explore three different forces that may affect what they look like.

Types of PlayTypes

Basic or singular playtypes

Play has been recognised as a heterogeneous phenomenon for some time. This means that the term 'play' is the overall heading for several sub-categories, which have become known as playtypes.

I wrote in Chapter One that Burghardt (1998), states that each of these 'playtypes' 'may have different causal bases, functions, phylogenies and ontogenies' (p. 6). That is, each one may:

- have been brought into existence by different factors;
- exist to do different things;
- have appeared at different points in evolutionary time;
- appear at different points in each child's development.

Over the years, there have been a number of different classifications of these playtypes. Burghardt (2005) states that

Parten (1932), for example, divided play into solitary independent play, interactive associative play (unorganised), and cooperative or organised play. Smilansky developed a scheme that subdivided play into functional, constructive, socio-dramatic and games with rules (p. 103)

Fagen (1995) put forward what Burghardt (2005) called a levels or grade hierarchy approach, categorising play mainly as different levels of social play, whilst Mitchell (1990) developed a scheme that was based on actions not movements. These actions he called 'autotelic, schematic, learned autotelic, teasing, mimetic, pretend and communicative pretend' (p. 108).

Other schemas have included categories like locomotor rotational, object, social, sensorimotor, construction, rough and tumble, language and make-believe play.

Each of these constructs has been developed from the observations of their creators, scientists who have spent many hours observing, categorising and analysing the behaviours we currently label as playtypes.

The basic material to construct *A Playworker's Taxonomy* was already there. What I had to do was find it, by undertaking a comprehensive trawl of the scientific literature to identify the different applications and then select those playtypes that made sense to me. I did so in terms of my own playwork diagnostic criteria – Intuition, childhood **M**emory, playwork **E**xperience and the scientific **E**vidence, described using the acronym IMEE. (This is more fully described in Hughes 1996b and 2001a.)

This personal route was unavoidable to me. It was an essential starting point if I was going to develop what I felt would be a playwork relevant taxonomy. The playtypes I eventually chose would have to faithfully reflect my perception of the whole range of children's play behaviour; both as I remembered it from my own childhood and as I had observed, through the prisms of parent and playworker. I appreciated that it would probably need to be fine-tuned, to have a similar impact on others, but the first port of call had to be my own experiences.

The scheme I eventually chose originally consisted of fifteen playtypes:

Communication, Creative, Deep, Dramatic, Exploratory, Fantasy, Imaginative, Locomotor, Mastery, Object, Recapitulative, Role, Rough and Tumble, Social, Socio-Dramatic, Symbolic

(Recapitulative Play was actually added when the second edition of the Taxonomy was created. See Chapters One and Three for my rationale.)

The scheme was bigger than the others mentioned above. It was experimental, even controversial, and unavoidably coloured by my own emotions and sensitivities. But it did feel holistic, authentic and representative, of the range of play experiences I had engaged in as a child, and had observed other children engaging in and, as such, was one of the most important criteria for its development; namely, that playworkers would recognise the categories I included.

However, there were some complications. For example, although Fantasy Play and Imaginative Play were represented separately in the literature, some playworkers found them difficult to separate both in practice and in the Taxonomy. Conway (2001) for example, described them as 'a sub-division too far', because, to some, it proved very difficult to provide adequate definitions and descriptions of them, that clearly articulated their differences.

The inclusion of other playtypes in the Taxonomy proved difficult for different reasons. For example, some playworkers felt that including Rough and Tumble Play might encourage racism, bullying or real fighting, whilst others judged that including Deep Play might result in children being badly injured or even killed.

Although I understood the concerns, I was not sure whether it was up to me to address them. The Taxonomy had been created to provide a comprehensive and accurate categorisation of playtypes. Hopefully, this had been achieved. That one or two might appear to merge, was a problem. But I thought that the categorisation would be solved as playworkers became more expert at distinguishing between them.

People's feelings about the effect of the inclusion of Rough and Tumble and Deep Play, was a different story. I had no wish to encourage bullying, racism or lethal accidents either, but neither did I believe that the inclusion of these playtypes would have this effect. My only response was, 'These are authentic types of play, they are as vital to a child's development as any other, and should be facilitated, where possible. If that sometimes creates problems, we have to solve the problems. We can't ban the playtypes!'

Further complications

However, some time after publication, a problem did arise that I thought needed to be addressed. Playworkers and trainers were contacting me saying that sometimes they were finding it difficult to decide what playtypes they were observing, particularly when the children they were watching were engaged in complicated and rapid routines, which was a lot of the time. 'They all seem to flow into one another,' people said.

My initial reaction was to revisit the original playtypes categorisation and see if anything could be done to simplify the situation. My first thought was that it might help if some way could be found to differentiate between the sixteen scientifically defined playtypes and what playworkers were seeing in practice, ensuring that they would not necessarily assume that everything they saw would fit neatly into the Taxonomy. For although the Taxonomy was comprehensive – perhaps too comprehensive – it only represented my selection of what scientists had observed, and that might be a weakness. The problem was that all too often, scientific observation, in controlled circumstances, or on other species, did not accurately reflect children's play as manifested in 'the wild' or in spaces specifically created for 'free play'. This was an issue that had regularly been brought up by researchers for at least twenty years.

The differentiating mechanism I chose was to give the sixteen a new collective label: a label that implicitly acknowledged that play *might* have more components than the 16 playtypes I had identified, whilst also distinguishing the sixteen from any new components that might be found. So, if further analysis did come up with alternatives or additions to the sixteen, then what I viewed as the scientific foundation of play – the sixteen basic play archetypes if you like – could still be used as the analytical starting point and not be rejected because problems with them were being encountered.

I chose to call the sixteen 'basic' or 'singular' playtypes. (I couldn't decide which, for reasons outlined in Chapter Six.) The term was intended to suggest, that irrespective of the confusion people were encountering, the sixteen still represented an indivisible base-line for playtypes.

Basic or Singular Playtypes	**Other Playtypes/Formats**
16 playtypes	???

This meant that, notwithstanding new theoretical or practical revelations about sub-dividing any of the sixteen, the names allocated to playtypes in the Taxonomy could still be used to describe the basic playtype units. However, I had already begun to accept that some change might be necessary. I had done some observations myself, and like other people, I was also noticing discrepancies between the descriptions listed in the Taxonomy and what I was seeing children doing.

This did not mean that the 'basic' playtypes were redundant; they were not. Although some of what children were observed doing did not fit tidily into the categories outlined in the Taxonomy, general observation of children's movements and their use of props, language and risk, still demonstrated that each of the 'basic' playtypes was identifiable in children's play and legitimate to use as a descriptor. The problem was not that the basic playtypes were not being observed, the problem was that we seemed to be observing something other than the sixteen playtypes.

However, no sooner had I chosen to call all sixteen basic playtypes 'basic', implying indivisibility, than that idea began to evolve and I began to imagine that each basic or singular playtype must contain a range of complexity, and ranges of modes of application for that playtype, perhaps the language equivalent of emphasis and nuance.

By this I meant that no playtype is manifested in just one repetitive, identical routine of behaviour and level of motivation. Children, environments and children's perceptions of environments, are all different, and change all the time. There could be a number of different manifestations of each basic playtype, created not only by the child's developmental stage, but also by minor variations in its physical and mental states (affector/s) at the time it was engaged in a particular playtype.

3D spectra

I wondered if it would help if these different playtypes affectors could be organised under a number of broad headings of their own, called 'spectra', to make it possible to estimate positions on scales of different affects.

Affector 1   Affector 2   Affector 3

PlayTypes manifestation =

Would this help playworkers to better describe what they were observing? Although it would veer descriptions away from the simple sixteen playtypes, I thought it might. However, any analysis of playtypes that required more than a simple observation would not be able to be conducted in the 'field' as such. For although diffi-culties arising from straightforward observations could be overcome with practice and more refined observational criteria, more detailed or advanced analysis could only be undertaken if the play behaviour was filmed or similarly recorded, and it is with this proviso that I offer the following possibility. There are at least three of these spectra, and each one would simultaneously be acting on the basic/singular playtype under observation, and go some way to creating some of the complexity people were encountering. For, as in 3D chess, each of these spectra was on a different plane, and each playtype could be manifesting aspects of each one. That is,

The playtype we observe = the sum of all active 3D spectra for that play-type.

The first of these I describe the 'Proto-types to Mature-types' Spectrum because it considers the effects of the child's developmen-tal stage on its ability to manifest playtypes.

The second I describe as the 'Hard to Soft' Spectrum, because it considers the effects of the child's perceived emotional state on its application of playtypes.

The third I describe as the 'Manifest to Latent' Spectrum because it considers the effects of the child's imagination on how visual its engagement in different playtypes would be.

I will explore each one in turn.

The 'Proto-types to Mature-types' Spectrum

The first spectrum is based upon the assumption that playtypes are formed over chronological time, and that babies and young children do not, or cannot, manifest 'full-blown' playtypes; that what we actually see during our observations of playtypes, could be age or development dependent and would be slightly different if the child were younger/older, or at a slightly different physical/cognitive developmental stage.

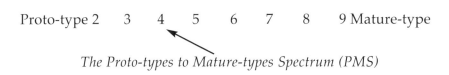

Proto-type 2   3   4   5   6   7   8   9 Mature-type

The Proto-types to Mature-types Spectrum (PMS)

Certainly in my own experience, a three-year-old is more able to engage in a recognisable form of Rough and Tumble Play, than say a two-year-old, but less able than say, an eight-year-old. Issues of size, strength, coordination, calibration, speed and so on, all play a part here. Similarly, the skills necessary for full-blown Locomotor Play also evolve over time.

The idea of cooperation inherent in Social Play takes time to comprehend and apply. The computations that make the prediction, calculation and planning of Mastery Play possible, take time to evolve. The abstract nature of Symbolism requires a capacity for conceptualisation and abstraction to have evolved. Deep Play needs highly evolved physical and psychic skills and judgements, to ensure that when children engage with real risk, they do so in combination with their best chances for survival. (This material can be confirmed in any comprehensive child-development text.)

Why is this? I said earlier that there appears to be a loop that operates during infancy and childhood between the embryonic brain and the environment, between brain growth and playing. If there is a relationship between early playful environmental interaction and brain growth, it will by definition, be less developed than at later developmental stages. By this I mean that simply because the brain is being formed by the movement and information-gathering capability of playing, there will be a stage when movements and brain are at least, comparatively primitive. That is to say, when relatively few cells and synapses are responsible for initiating simple and uncoordinated movements.

This situation will change continually as more cells and synapses are formed, and more information/experiences enable movement and stimulus and object discrimination skills to develop. However, I still suggest that it will take time – let's say up to eight years, if applying the sensitive period hypothesis is appropriate – before embryonic playtypes have become fully mature, full-blown playtypes.

Although the sixteen playtypes described in the Taxonomy relate to full-blown playtypes at around the age of 7–8 years, we can see their proto-types forming much earlier, as younger children attempt to undertake the early stages of one or other of the basic playtypes.

Recently, I observed a group of children of different ages, clustered around a number of hanging ropes. During their dynamic with one another, they began to interact on a variety of levels with the ropes. The younger children tried to jump up and hang on to them and, if they managed that, they engaged in short rudimentary swinging movements. Older children engaged in much more complex swinging movements, this incorporated a longer length of time; climbing up the rope; using the rope to swing onto a platform, and so on. However, on walking into one of the ropes, one of the older children began spontaneously to engage in a complex routine in which the rope appeared to be cast as a protagonist. The child bumped into the rope, which made the rope move. This seemed enough of a stimulus for the child to engage in a mock fight with the rope that entailed the child in sophisticated 'boxing' and 'kickboxing' movements that included dodging, feinting, punching and kicking. None of the younger children engaged with anything like this level of sophistication.

The 'Hard to Soft' Spectrum

My second spectrum assumes that at every stage of playtypes development, children are applying their current emotional state, where the manifestation at one end of the hard/soft spectrum is both intended and perceived as relatively positive, perhaps as gentle, whilst at the other end, the manifestation is both intended and perceived as rougher or relatively more negative. This is most easily explained again using overtly physical playtypes, like Rough and Tumble Play, or Locomotor Play.

Rough and Tumble Play for example, can incorporate routines from gentle wrestling (soft) to quite vigorous mock combat (hard), and from gentle tickling (soft) to forceful pinning down (hard). Locomotor Play can be similarly manifested. Games of tag or football can range from relaxed (soft) to vigorous (hard).

Soft   2   3   4   5   6   7   8   9   Hard

The Hard to Soft Spectrum

The Hard to Soft spectrum can also be applied to the more abstract playtypes. For example, Creative Play can incorporate anything from doodling (soft) to the application of the skills of composition, colour choice and so on (hard).

Symbolic Play can also be analysed in terms of its Hard to Soft spectrum. Symbolic Play can be manifested using a doll to represent an animal or person (soft), or a flag, representing a deeply held emotional stance, like patriotism (hard).

Object Play can exist on a spectrum ranging from the cursory handling of an object (soft), where the child may simply be logging the object's tactile qualities, to complex manipulations: for example, a Rubik Cube, or a camera (hard), where the child needs to apply the skills of concentration and deduction.

The extremes are comparatively simple to interpret, although unified criteria would need to be established. The major interpretive problem, and this probably applies equally to each of the spectra, occurs when we move away from the extremes and observe a hard/soft mix of varying degrees of hardness or softness. Whilst we might pitch fire-lighting towards the hard extreme of Mastery Play, where, for example, would we pitch kite flying?

Or in terms of Socio-Dramatic Play, is shouting harder or softer than screaming or throwing a tantrum? If this type of tool has any worth, these kinds of questions will need to be asked, attempts made to test the answers, and conclusions justified.

If nothing else, this demonstrates how complex play and children are, and how far we can move – in theory – away from simplistic overviews of what they are doing and what are their intentions.

The 'Manifest to Latent' Spectrum

My final spectrum provides a rudimentary tool for analysing play-types in terms of their visibility or not. Like the other two spectra, the 'Manifest to Latent' Spectrum will require the development of judgement and practice. In the case of this spectrum, specifically, it should also be acknowledged that because we cannot know what children are thinking, our view can only be totally subjective.

That having been said, being able to provide an albeit subjective assessment of a playtype's symbolic, imaginative or fantasy content, for example, is only useful when attempting to convey a comprehensive impression of what is being observed.

Manifest Components 5 4 3 2 1 0 1 2 3 4 5 Latent Components

The Manifest to Latent Spectrum

This will also help us to assess whether a child's play is symptomatic of that which might be displayed by someone showing some distortion as a consequence of say, acute play deprivation. (If, for example, a child appears to be playing continually in an imaginary mode, isolated, communicating with the invisible and showing other abnormal traits.) We could check this against, for example, templates of the Proto-types to Mature-types Spectrum, to have some idea of what we should be able to expect of a child of its age, or at its particular developmental stage.

What can we do with information we gain from spectra analysis?

The short answer is, not a lot – yet! As I write, I am concerned that I am only making the situation more, rather than less, confused. However, playwork does have a problem. If we want/need to be able accurately to describe what children do when they play – for the practical purposes of more accurate modification regimes, or even clinical diagnosis – it may not be enough to simply say that they engage in playtypes, or in this or that specific playtype.

Certainly, such speculation will tell us something about the range of play experiences children are accessing. It will also tell us if children are biasing their experience towards one or more playtypes. However, that is all.

What we still do not know is the detail or what we might be able to do with this information. What, for example, are the adaptational implications of different spectral permutations? Do most children manifest more or less the same spectra positions with age and, if not, why not? Does playwork environmental modification make shifts occur in spectra, when children's own choice of environments doesn't, or vice versa? If playwork is attempting to support the adaptation process by facilitating one of its most important mechanisms, play, will a construct of spectra help or hinder that?

Then there is the whole can of ethical worms about 'Health Intervention'. For example, what spectral construct would we expect from a child in terms of its anticipated developmental stage? The Proto-types to Mature-types Spectrum could provide playwork with a comparative guide.

What does it tell us if, say, a four-year-old child's play analysis is more Mature than Proto, more Soft than Hard, and more Manifest than Latent? Does it give us an indication of the child's mental or physical well-being and/or adaptability? Could it help us to forecast strengths or weaknesses that could be addressed by exposure to other experiences? Should this even be a consideration?

At this stage in our exploration of playtypes, all we can say safely is that it may present us with more rudimentary data on the perceived nature of playtypes. What we do with our interpretations will have to be the subject of thought and research in the future

In Chapters Six and Seven we continue this discussion.

Chapter Six

Differentiating the sixteen basic or singular playtypes from what could be termed 'background noise', could be helpful in observations of play. It would mean that if the observer was simply trying to focus on playtypes as specified in the Taxonomy, then much of what would be seen could be simply disregarded on the grounds of non-compliance to the 'basic' play-types criteria. It would also mean that what was being monitored could then be analysed for its relative maturity of exposition, its affective inten-sity and its perceived symbolic, imaginative or fantasy content, as outlined in Chapter Five: all of which could be useful in assessing the facilitating potential of a playspace, and the play literacy and dexterity of the children using such space.

However, what if the background noise, the 'merging', as I have termed it, was actually the manifestation of other, even more intricate playtypes than those classified in the Taxonomy? What if, in middle or late childhood for example, as they perceived a desire to have a hobby, or learn to defend themselves or have relationships, children's basic playtypes tended to combine, to merge with one another, to become amalgamated playtypes – playtypes that would allow for more intricate behaviour and whose combined efficacy might be more than the sum of each of the playtypes being merged? (In Chapter Five, I found myself referring to 'basic' play-types as 'singular', because I had realised that playtypes might exist that were made up of two, three or more of these basic playtypes.)

What if we were able to 'see' the background noise and 'name' it, in the same way as we have 'named' our basic playtypes? Not only would we be able to collect much more data than we currently can, we would also be able to categorise what we observe, in a hierarchy of perceived complexity and ontological manifestation.

Thus for the purposes of a more comprehensive observation and identification of play and playtypes, perhaps a fruitful route to supplement that taken in the previous chapter would also be to anticipate playtypes as blocks that join together to form larger groups, as well as expecting singular playtypes to be manifested in children's play. These groups may have the added advantage of being more intelligible as normal play behaviour, than their singular counterparts.

Amalgamated PlayTypes

Do singular playtypes join together to become the individual components of even more intricate behavioural routines, routines, which we might call 'amalgamated playtypes'? Does engaging in the sixteen singular playtypes provide the player with the foundation of movement and thought that makes the more elaborate movements and thoughts implied by 'amalgamated playtypes', possible and likely?

Could basic/singular playtypes be the engines for brain and muscle development and the processes that actually use the resulting enlarged muscular and neural capacities to facilitate the amalgamation of playtypes? Could they be involved in the production of neural and muscle tissue *and* in determining how it is eventually used?

Sutton-Smith (1997), citing Gould (1996) and Kotulak (1996), offers an interesting passage with respect to this. He writes, 'Humans do not contain anywhere near enough genes to make enough individual cells to create a fully operational brain, so an overabundance of the same or similar cells and synapses is produced, and then the brain has to use them to make itself work.' What does Sutton-Smith mean?

Burghardt (1998) presented evidence (from other authors)

suggesting that 'play behaviour in some juvenile mammals may permanently modify muscle fibre differentiation and cerebella synapse distribution ... the changes posited are permanent and unlikely to be induced by other behavioural means' (p. 18).

This demonstrates that play impacts upon brain and muscle growth, and implies that after a period of play a child will have more neural and muscle tissue than it would have had previously. What I draw from this and from Sutton-Smith is that this play-induced neural material may be that overabundance of cells and synapses to which Sutton-Smith refers.

What happens to this expanded neural capacity? The brain has to use it to make itself work (Kotulak 1996 in Sutton-Smith 1997, p. 223).

This is an intriguing idea. But how does the brain use this over-abundance of cells and synapses to do this?

Sutton-Smith argues that play's role could be in the 'actualisation of brain potential' – making connections real, rather than possible – 'its function being to save ... more of the variability that is potentially there, than would otherwise be saved if there were no play' (pp. 225–6).

My understanding of Sutton-Smith's (and other sources he cites) argument, is firstly, that the human child develops a huge neuronal over-capacity, which will die if it is not used. This neuronal over-capacity has resulted from playing. i.e. the act of playing has actually stimulated the production of neuronal material. Secondly, what he seems to be implying is that playing not only *produces* this material, but more play *'actualises'* it, i.e. transforms it from func-tionless matter, into matter with a function. Its function, if I infer from Sutton-Smith's speculation correctly, is to memorise or facili-tate play, either by being imprinted with transitory, spontaneous, goalless play routines (or imbued with fragments of cortical play maps (Brown 1998) that are disbursed throughout the over-capac-ity) as a way of saving 'more of the variability that is potentially there, than would otherwise be saved ...'. What Sutton-Smith appears to be saying is that play is being used as a mechanism for retaining the neural flexibility of play, as opposed to the inflexibility it would acquire if it had a permanent job, as a way of ensuring it has adaptive capacity when the need arises. This would be a vital weapon in the organism's fight against extinction.

He continues, 'quirky, [apparently] redundant and flexible' responses to experience, i.e. play, 'result in the uptake of this over capacity, thus ensuring its continued participation in future brain processes, and avoiding problems which Gould suggested were associated with 'rigidification of behaviour after any future successful adaptation' (Sutton-Smith, ibid., p. 231; Brown 1998, p. 253).

So, first of all the child plays and *produces* an overcapacity of brain material. Then the child plays and the result is that the overcapacity of brain material is transformed into actualised (useable) neural material that can participate in the playful activity of the brain, until it is required for adaptive needs. This means that play is acting on two levels simultaneously: 1. In the production of new brain material and; 2. In the actualisation of brain material produced earlier. Although this actualised material is in a state whose function is not yet finalised, it can be incorporated into the brain function proper and will not die because it has not been used.

However, this could mean that the play behaviour we observe is simply the manifestation of the increasing levels or ranges of the flexible behaviour we need to facilitate adaptation and stave off extinction. In effect, that play's sole job is to hold neural material in readiness for its real job, adaptation, and that play has no function other than that.

It may have been the case when play was first evolving that this was its only purpose. However, I think play has been selected by evolution, over the millennia, because it represents a coming together of several powerful factors – the period we call childhood, no preconceptions, physical and psychological flexibility, a neophilic drive – factors that make it incredibly multifunctional. Play can create brain and muscle tissue, it can provide a job for that tissue, which it has turned out is itself very useful to the organism –

like providing it with a 'consciousness' (Brown 1998, p. 254), and a whole range of skills that make our actual existence more interesting and 'deep'. All these factors tend to make me think that they are contributory to a particular neuroludic-evolutionary theoretical construct.

A hierarchy of perceived complexity and ontological manifestation

Therefore, I think it is reasonable to speculate that the development of flexible neural material and quirky, flexible play behaviours, which seem to run in parallel, could reflect a gradual complication of playtypes over time.

My proposition is that basic/singular playtypes could 'merge' to form the more generic behaviours, in which we all see children engaging. In fact, if, as was being suggested at the beginning of this chapter, play acts on numerous levels to provide the underpinning hierarchy of neural and muscular development for increasingly complex evolutionary transcendences (as reflected in play) then there is also a logic to the suggestion that there are proto-playtypes, i.e. playtypes can be broken down into their component parts; that singular playtypes may themselves represent the proto-forms of more intricate behaviours. That, however, is another story.

Amalgamated playtypes

What the previous passages are attempting to provide is an analysis of the increasing intricacy that would be necessary as play facilitated brain growth and analysed novel information. If, at the neuronal/synaptic level, play is engaged in processes of increasing sophistication, that 'sophistication' might also be reflected at a behavioural level and it would be visible.

Observing children playing as mentioned in Chapter Five, one is struck not only with the speed with which they play and move between singular playtypes, but how difficult it is to record the actual playtypes they are engaged in, and how much easier it would be to describe the child's play routines in terms of more amalgamated headings, where, at least from a playwork perspective, recognisable everyday children's game and activity names might replace the singular titles.

Look, for example, at the game of tag. To follow a game of this nature and attempt to log behaviour as it moves flawlessly from one singular playtype to another, often for many minutes, is difficult, if not impossible to do. To be able to simply write 'Tag' for a time period, in the knowledge that the term 'Tag' was simply an amalgamating term for a group of predicted and re-occurring singulars, would make certain kinds of analyses much simpler.

A game of tag contains more or less the same singulars, although not necessarily in the same quantities or order. To posses those data would require a singular analysis. If, for example, our question was a more general one – how many games of tag do the children play in a day and how long do they last? – then it would simply require the construction of an amalgamated singular template for 'Tag' and data could be collected and an analysis conducted.

If for argument's sake we say that tag always contains an amalgamation of the following singulars:

Social + 3D Gross + Locomotor + Communication + Recapitulative + Deep

We can then analyse the tag that is manifested in the playspace to check this assumption. If it is found to be correct, then the level and duration of tag, as an amalgamation of those playtypes, can be measured and analysed. It may even be found that the proportions of particular singulars is roughly always the same. In other words, by timing the duration of an amalgamated episode, we may be able to give an approximation of the dispersal of each component singular.

Similarly, we could say that playing with dolls contains an amalgamation of these singulars:

Communication + Deep + Imaginative + Recapitulative + Social + Symbolic

Having confirmed that that is the case, we can simply observe children playing with dolls and provide an analysis from that perspective.

The great beauty of this from a playwork perspective is that the playworker is released from the 'singular' hegemony, which without greater observational skills and sophisticated filming equipment is very difficult to analyse, and instead is faced with analysing familiar and recognisable routines that have a time-span and that are, to some extent, at least, predictable in their form.

It is simply a matter of getting the initial amalgamation analysis correct. This would obviously take time, but it may only have to be done once, rather than at every observation.

Let us look at two other familiar examples before we move on. Look at how intricate they are. It is no wonder that we are having problems observing their singular components.

Look at painting, for example.

Object + Creative + Symbolic + Communication + Deep + Exploratory +
Fantasy + Imaginative + Mastery + Recapitulative + others

In this form it is complicated enough. But imagine if we were then to overlay a singular analysis of it with a spectra one too?

And what about football?

Gross Locomotor + Social + Communication + Deep + Mastery + Object +
Recapitulative + Symbolic + Rough and Tumble

Given the speed with which the game is conducted, the intensity of the interaction between the players and between the players and the ball, it is little wonder that the problems of observation and analysis seem insurmountable.

Whether we see games, pastimes and activities as amalgamated playtypes, is probably neither here nor there, as long as we are aware both of play's complexity and that everything we play at is made up of one or more basic components we call playtypes: playtypes which must be able to manifest themselves in playspaces, if the more complex games that they may make up are to be able to exist. In other words, we have to value and provide for the individual pieces of the jigsaw, or the jigsaw in total will not be able to come together.

Merging playtypes

One way of demonstrating the intricacy of amalgamated playtypes especially if/when they occur in conjunction with the same or other amalgams, is to view it as a dance in which different individuals are undertaking the same or different moves. There is a choreographic feel about the dynamic of a playspace that leaves the observer wondering how children are able to navigate the space and the activity within it, without becoming casualties of what seems, after all, what Battram (2002) called the 'edge of recalcitrance'. Not chaos, and not *not* chaos, but something verging on the edge of chaos. How do children know how to operate at this level?

There is a very interesting contribution in Beckoff and Byers' (1998) *Animal Play*, entitled 'Intentional communication and social play', that provides some interesting insights into the possible answer to this question.

Quoting Gopnik (1993), among others, the authors, Beckoff and Allen (1998), imply that children do not consciously know how to navigate the edge of chaos, but that their whole body is constructed to know what is going on and how to avoid or interact with it. It is as if, as they are playing, they have developed a way of knowing where their own limbs are in relation to everything around them and also where are those of any others in close proximity.

> … we innately map the body movements of others onto our own kinaesthetic sensations. This initial bridge between inside and outside, the self and other, underlies our later conviction that all mental states are things both we and others share. (Gopnik 1993, p. 110)

It is as if each child knows what the other is going to do, because in the same situation, that is what they would have done. Beckoff and Allen (1998) elaborate further:

> … certain kinds of information that come, literally from inside ourselves is coded in the same way as information that comes from observing the behaviour of others. Gopnik (1993) claims that other's body movements are mapped onto one's own kinaesthetic sensations, based on [the] prior experiences of the observer. (p. 110)

What we might be observing, when we look at different playtypes is the result of a 'phylogenetically' ancient scheme of movement, that makes it possible for children to forecast the place in space that others might occupy, and what they might be feeling whilst they are there.

Again this supports the assertion made by Sturrock, in Hughes (2001b, p. 22), that whilst even trained and experienced playworkers might find it difficult, if not impossible, to untangle what is happening in a particularly complicated play bout, children intuitively know what is going on. 'Children are the sophisticates,' he said, 'and it is we [adults] who are the primitives.'

Before we leave amalgamated playtypes, I want to return briefly to the Gopnik quote above referring to the bridge between inside and outside.

Play as an auric/neural interfacer

What makes both Sutton-Smith's and others' contributions above even more fascinating, is that like Gopnik (1993), they also imply that play can operate both inside and outside the body. In the case of the Sutton-Smith material, my interpretation is that play is operational both in the physical formation of INTERNAL tissue, and at the same time in giving that tissue an EXTERNAL function, in this case, facilitating more complex play routines.

It does appear from what Sutton-Smith, Gould, Kotulak and now

Gopnik seem to be suggesting, is that during its development and application of neural tissue, play is acting as a bi-medium interfacer, similar to that suggested in Hughes (1999a); that one of play's vital early functions is the creation of a Sub Operating System. (For a full discussion, see Hughes 1999a.)

The gist of that argument was that play acts as an interface or conduit between outside the child (the physical environment) and inside the child, (brain, muscle etc.), between external reality and the individual's brain/senses. In much the same way as an operating system in a computer provides an interface between the computer's hard disc and any software. That as the child's play behaviour affects the external environment, so the affected external environment impacts on the complexity of the child's play behaviour and, as a consequence, on the child's brain and muscles, in a continuing cycle.

For example

$$\text{Output} \quad \rightarrow \rightarrow$$

Brain/ Muscle (Senses)   Environment (Reality)

$$\leftarrow \leftarrow \text{Input}$$

This would suggest that play is able to operate as an interface between two different mediums: physical matter, i.e. neural tissue; and energy, i.e. sensory stimuli and information, as what might be termed an auric/neural interfacer.

This is a difficult idea to rationalise if play is seen only as behaviour. If play is conceptualised initially as energy packets (quanta?), which can be manifested either as behaviour or as adaptations/changes at a cellular, molecular, atomic or at an even more discrete level – which is what is happening to brain and muscle tissue anyway – then visualising play as a modifier of visually less tangible areas, the interface between matter and energy, for example, becomes less difficult, making it easier for us to comprehend the simultaneous interplay between numerous amalgamated playtypes. This is yet another stepping off point for an evolving neuroludic-evolutionary theory.

Whatever the eventual outcome of playtypes theorising, the integration of basic playtypes to make more complex playtypes is not the only possibility, as we will see in Chapter Seven.

PART III

Chapter Seven

Reflecting on the source, visible manifestations and functions of playtypes provides us with numerous alternatives of what might be called 'Complex PlayTypes'. This final chapter discusses some of them, and begins a discussion about what children's contemporary playtypes might represent and symbolise.

As I have cited on numerous occasions (Hughes 1996, 2000, 2001) Sturrock suggests that there is a sense in which every playful manifestation is symbolic, as we have no proof of either what motivates or creates their appearance.

However, applying my own reflective template, IMEE (Hughes 1996b; see Chapter Five) has led me to speculate on a number of different although related ideas about Complex PlayTypes, about what gives them their unique look and function.

Although the creation of any kind of definitive analysis from this would be far too optimistic, reflection on these ideas will hopefully have the effect of initiating debate and moving thinking forward.

Further PlayTypes Complexities

In Chapter One I outlined some ideas that introduce the subject of Complex PlayTypes.

The triune brain

In the early 1960s, the neuroscientist Paul MacLean put forward the hypothesis that the human brain has evolved as a triune brain. That is, three different neural structures in one (MacLean 1973). He suggested that deep within the structure we call the brain is what he called the reptilian complex, or Rc. This entity, which he suggests is responsible for our reflex/instinctive behaviour, consists mainly of the basal ganglia area of the brain.

Enveloping the reptilian complex is the limbic system – primarily consisting of 'the hippocampus, the hypothalamus, and the thalamus, but also the pituitary gland, which has been aptly described as the conductor of the endocrine orchestra' (Stevens and Price 2000, p. 16). The limbic system is said to be responsible for both our emotional interface and behaviour. Enveloping them both is the neocortex, which is said to be responsible for our rational behaviour.

MacLean's theory suggests that our oldest ancestors, reptiles, evolved ways of behaving and perceiving that were neither rational nor emotional, but which relied on reflex 'fight and flight' reactions to events. Their brain, the reptilian complex or Rc, mediated a spontaneous reaction to the world in a defensive, protective and primarily survivally-orientated manner, which reflected its overriding needs at the time. We can still recognise these traits both within ourselves, and within the children with whom we work.

Over evolutionary time, a new neural layer evolved to address the needs of our evolving predecessors in new circumstances, and the limbic layer was born. Over time, a reptilian organism whose only relationship with the world appeared aggressive, gradually mutated into an ape-like organism, which because of the newly evolved limbic layer, gave rise to an emotional creature; one that, although still retaining its earlier spontaneous fight/flight reactions to the world, was more able to feel and to acknowledge that other organisms, its young, for example, also had feelings. We can recognise these as general human characteristics.

Eventually, probably after many hundreds of thousands of years, this emotional/primitive repto-primate mutated into what we humans have become today, and the third part of MacLean's neural construct, the neocortex, gradually evolved. Suddenly, a creature that had only been able to react to events, was, as Stevens and Price (2000) wrote 'conscious, voluntary and rational' (p. 17) and was now able to think, consider and reflect on events, was able to develop and amend strategies as conditions changed and became, to some extent, the orchestrator of its own destiny.

It has been widely accepted for many years that the human brain evolved from a comparatively simple structure at the beginning of evolutionary time to its current complex form, and that the structure of the contemporary human brain corresponds with MacLean's model. What is different about the MacLean idea is the notion of the complete 'separateness' of each evolved segment, as stated by Stevens and Price (2000).

each with a different phylogenetic history, each with its own special intelligence, its own special memory, its own sense of time and space, and its own motor functions. (p. 15)

Or as MacLean (1985) states in a later paper,

Radically different in their chemistry and structure and in an evolutionary sense, aeons apart. (p. 219)

This suggests that the human brain, presents the human being with a view of existence that not only spans evolutionary and phyloge-netic time, but also appears to give support to Grof's (1975) trans-species ideas. It may also give rise to what Stevens and Price (ibid.) term the 'triune mind' (p. 18) too, where the human view of the world, and the behaviour that results from it, is affected by distinctly non-human chemistry and ancient ecological memories.

However, although each of these 'brains', retains its own 'full functional integrity' (p. 14), or to put it another way, each of the 'three [distinct] central processing assemblies, or decision-making units, ... responds in its characteristic way to changes in the environment ... [their] activity is to some extent co-ordinated' (p. 19).

In the MacLean triune model of the brain, we are looking at a neural structure that may sometimes behave as one unified brain, at other times as three separate brains, and at others as three distinct combinations of two of the components – i.e. Rc/limbic, Rc/neocortex, and limbic/neocortex. Not three different behavioural possibilities but seven!

This is all very interesting, but what has it got to do with playtypes and playwork practice? Well, in Chapter One I posed two questions relating to playtypes. I asked whether:

1. individual playtypes might be located in specific sections of this triune brain, i.e. the reptilian section, the limbic section or the neocortex section?
2. each playtype might have three different versions or components?

Let us look briefly at each of these questions.

1. Might individual playtypes be located in specific sections of this triune brain, i.e. the reptilian section, the limbic section or the neocortex section?

After reflecting on the nature of the different groupings, I arrived at a theoretical distribution that revealed an interesting evolutionary spread to the order in which playtypes might have evolved throughout the triune brain. A distribution that allows us to make guesses at the prevailing astronomical, or meteorological or atmospheric circumstances, which may have actually caused or accompanied their appearance many years ago.

Reptilian Complex *(Reflex)* = Deep, Exploratory, Locomotor, Object, Rough and Tumble.

Limbic *(Emotional)* = Creative, Dramatic, Fantasy, Imaginative, Socio-Dramatic, Role.

Neocortex (*Rational*) = Communication, Recapitulative, Social, Mastery, Symbolic.

The distribution was made by looking at each of the sixteen playtypes from the perspective of its potential contribution either to the organism's survival (Reflex), to its potential as an emotional or expressive medium (Emotional), or to its possible role as a social or cultural mechanism (Rational).

Playtypes which evolved during the period of Rc evolution might have been the more relatively exploratory and outgoing of the group, i.e. Deep, Exploratory, Locomotor, Object, Rough and Tumble. Those that evolved as emotional manifestations of the limbic system, might be softer and expressive and could include Creative, Dramatic, Fantasy, Imaginative, Socio-Dramatic and Role. Those that were the more social or cultural manifestations of the neocortex, might include Communication, Recapitulative, Social, Mastery and Symbolic. Obviously, this classification is pretty arbitrary, based as it is on theoretical speculation, but it does give us a context within which to begin to imagine when and even why particular playtypes may have evolved at all.

2. Might each playtype have three different versions?

Could each of the three parts of the Triune Brain have its own version of each of the sixteen playtypes and, if so, how might they manifest themselves? Let us explore this question using Locomotor Play as our example.

If each of the three parts of MacLean's Triune Brain had its own version of Locomotor Play then we can propose that:

Reptilian Complex Locomotor Play, would manifest itself as instinctive, unemotional and spontaneous attack and defence movements. This might begin to explain why some children engage in what appear to be unprovoked sociopathic attacks on other children and are unable to provide any satisfactory justification for having done so.

Limbic Locomotor Play would be driven by affect and would manifest itself in the aesthetic experiences of movement, like aerobics, ballet and the beautiful free running of the parkouristes. Locomotor Play in childhood is more than just movement. It is an exhilarating experience of near flight, of effortless calibration and stunning fun-filled gymnastics.

Neocortex Locomotor Play would be characterised by discipline and rules and would specialise in the efficiency and efficacy of the kinds of movements we might see in organised sports. It would be structured, require dedication and practice and would probably be described less as fun than as satisfying.

Given that play has a physiological impact on the construction of different areas of the brain (Burghardt 1998; Byers 1998), might it be that different behavioural subdivisions, i.e. playtypes, facilitate the construction of specific neural areas of the brain, or in specific brains, if we consider the triune model (Hughes 2006)? To be able to engage or not in Locomotor Play which is specifically reptilian or limbic or neocortical would have neurological implications for the genesis of synapses and cells in that particular part of the brain.

Mutants and isotopes

Whatever playtypes are for and whenever they have evolved, they are what they are. But how did they become what they are? This next section turns our gaze onto the circumstances under which playtypes may have evolved and asks: are today's playtypes simply updated versions of the originals (mutations), or are they variations on a theme for different conditions (isotopes)?

Contemporary playtypes as mutations

An evolutionary analysis of playtypes takes singular playtypes (Chapter Five), which as we have seen may themselves be hugely complex, onto another dimension, into evolutionary time, across the species, within the individual development of each child and into the cosmic arena. For what the two examples above reveal, is that once we begin to explore the phenomenon of playtypes in the context of the evolutionary process, it becomes almost impossible not to consider, theoretically, that the development and nature of playtypes may have been affected by any number of bio-evolutionary variables, including Phylogenic, Transpersonal, Ontogenic and Metaphysical factors.

For example:

The following categories may have impacted on the Phylogenic nature of playtypes:

Pre-human environs
Prehistoric environs
Stone Age environs
Iron Age
Bronze Age
Agrarian Age
Industrial Age

Whilst these categories may have impacted on the Transpersonal nature of playtypes:

Cultural
Artistic
Geographic
Culinary
Clothes / artefacts
Toys
Senses

These categories may have affected the Ontogenic structure and nature of playtypes:

Postnatal playtypes
Infancy
Toddlers/early years
Middle childhood
Late childhood
Adolescence

and these factors may have affected the Metaphysical nature of playtypes:

Time
Space
The Cosmos
The meaning of life
The permanence of death
Religions
God/gods

The following diagrams track two possible developmental routes for a playtype in the context of these variables.

Diagram One

<u>Original PlayType</u>   <u>Contemporary Mutation</u>

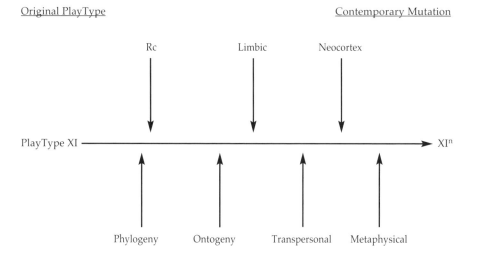

Diagram One describes the changes a playtype must survive over evolutionary time, as it is continually modified by the collective experiences of the human organisms that have hosted it to date. Each facet of experience, perhaps for millions of years, has chipped away at the manner in which it engages with the reality with which it interfaces, requiring constant modification in order to retain its maximum effective adaptive contribution. This supposes an enormous adaptive potential on the part of the playtype, which could be exerted on the playing organism. From this perspective, today's playtypes could be viewed as gradual mutations from the original (X1) – which have been engaged in a continuous dynamic of adaptation as experience and the host environment changes – to the form we see today, X1n.

Contemporary playtypes as isotopes

An alternative to the model proposed in Diagram One, is that instead of the development of a single contemporary mutation from the original playtype over evolutionary time, playtypes that vary slightly from the original are produced to address particular situations as circumstances change. This would mean that there would be numerous, perhaps minute variations of each playtype: variations that were able to address particular conditions, which have already arisen in evolutionary time and which could arise again at any time in the future.

Diagram Two

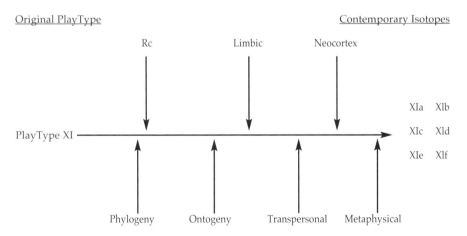

Diagram Two describes a different journey for our playtypes: that although experience may have an adaptive impact – as proposed in Diagram One – the primary, i.e. the main playtype adaptor, is the force that exerts the most influence on the organism during a particular period in evolutionary time, and by so doing, necessitates the creation of an isotopic version of the original which, whilst retaining most of the original's characteristics, has the signature of the individual force (Triune Brain, Phylogeny, etc.) as the dominant adaptive characteristic. As conditions change so the dominant adaptive force will also change, necessitating further new adaptive isotopes of the original to evolve.

One conclusion we can draw from these speculations is that if the process alluded to in Diagram One was the pattern followed by playtypes evolution, then there are still currently only sixteen playtypes. However, if the process alluded to in Diagram Two is more likely to have been the developmental pattern, then the real number of playtypes displayed in a child's play repertoire will be a function of the number of playtypes, times the number of variables one considers has been influential.

PlayTypes mutants and isotopes and playwork practice

Does it matter whether playtypes have evolved as mutants or isotopes of their originals, or neither? I think it does. We know that providing for play is not *just* about the creation of environments and services that facilitate play. It is also about ensuring that those environments and services created do actually address the phenomenon of play and not some socially convenient construct. Being clearer about the potential complexities of playing is essential to any comprehensive provision strategy.

Needless to say, this speculative analysis is onerous both in its complexity and volume. However, it is likely that we already subconsciously include many of these variables in what we observe and intuit when we facilitate children playing. After all they are not a separate species and we will also have the same or similar evolutionary currents running through us.

Having said that, more reflection and research still needs to be directed towards this area, if playwork is to feel the level of confidence it needs when making provision for these diverse and intricate phenomena.

The triune brain revisited

One final speculation regarding the possible sources and functions of playtypes remains to be explored. Playtypes may act as the visible manifestation of what C.G. Jung called 'archetypes'. If this is the case, then an understanding of how playtypes manifest themselves might help playworkers to make judgements about the health and well-being of those manifesting them.

Archetypes may have been being created in the human psyche since the dawn of time. They are regarded as encapsulating or drawn from the most primitive needs of all mankind. There could be as many archetypes as there are needs. Definition of specific archetypes as described by Jung are sparse, but one might imagine that they would include categories like gods and spirits, love and attachment, fertility rites, warfare, death, myth making, rituals and so on.

Jung proposed that every human being possesses an archetypal endowment of 'neuropsychic units' of the phylogenetic psyche (Stevens and Price 2000, p. 6). Archetypes have accumulated throughout our evolutionary history and perhaps, represent fundamental human psychic needs, or deep responses to cosmic or other catastrophes that may have happened long ago.

> each of which prepares us for the natural life-cycle of our species in the natural world in which we evolved. (Stevens and Price, ibid., p. 6)

As the human child passes through its various developmental stages, so these deep 'needs/memories' become an active component of its personality and its behaviour.

Jung called the human propensity for archetypes the 'collective unconscious', and it is suggested (Stevens and Price, ibid., p. 18) that their genesis is sourced in phylogenetically ancient parts of the brain. In the basal ganglia or the limbic system, if we apply MacLean's (1973) triune model.

Jung's thesis was that 'the purpose of life is the fullest realisation of the [individual] "archetypal programme"' (Stevens and Price, ibid., p. 7). As different archetypes or groups of archetypes become active at different points in a child's development, so they would impact upon the world around the child in their own unique way, their successful expression resulting in what Stevens and Price termed the 'fulfilment of archetypal intent' (p. 6) The result would be an individual who was psychically healthy, because these ancient and urgent needs were being met. Thus, if the children with whom playworkers come into contact in play situations are happy and balanced, it may be because their archetypal needs are being met through the comprehensive experience of their play.

However, if for some reason the [play] environment is unable to meet or accommodate an individual's particular archetypal needs at any given time, then that individual would feel unfulfilled, and the resulting 'frustration of archetypal intent' (Stevens 1982) will 'result in psychopathology' (Stevens and Price, ibid., p. 7).

Although expressed differently, this is much the same interpretation as has been given to the existence and activation of playtypes (Hughes 2004, 2005, 2006). That is to say, that playtypes have evolved as a response to massive, potentially species extinguishing events in the history of human evolution – perhaps too in other playing species – and that the opportunity to express or to satisfy them is crucial both to human sanity and to our capacity to withstand the pressures of extinction.

It has been consistently proposed (Hughes 2004, 2005, 2006) that the regular satisfactory expression of each playtype would result in a stable and grounded individual, whereas, a lack of that fulfilment, i.e. 'the frustration of playtype or of ludic intent', to paraphrase Stevens and Price's term, would result in 'many thousands of years of anticipated groundedness, adaptation and playful mutation crashing down around the child ... and it would be propelled into a state of … cosmic isolation, where literally nothing made sense any more' (Hughes 2003).

Consider for example, the fate of architectural student and mass murderer Stuart Whitman whose abusive and play-deprived childhood resulted in almost total playlessness – i.e. $\cong$ 100% play deprivation (Brown 1998). As a consequence it was concluded that he was rendered unable to devise survival strategies to deal with the abuse he experienced, and at a neural level, was totally unequipped 'to roll with the punches associated with daily social interactions' (Siviy 1998). He was eventually driven to express what I believe was his 'frustration of playtypes intent' by killing seventeen students and wounding thirty-one others (Beckoff and Byers 1998, p. 246).

This extreme example of the impact of the non-satisfaction of deep evolutionary needs, serves to demonstrate the total despair that might be felt by those unable to manifest, or play-out, archetypal propensities, either directly as playtypes, or through the medium of playtypes: the loneliness and lack of connection to a world and a reality that most of us take for granted. Psychiatrists call the resultant state 'psychopathology', i.e. mental illness, but in a sense this is less an illness, than the anticipated psychic state one might expect in any individual chronically experiencing playlessness for many years without letup. (See also Deprivation – Chapter Four.)

This model of playtypes as conduits for, or physical manifestations of, archetypes gives us an insight into the sensitivity of the human organism to a whole range of factors which most of us either take for granted or deny as important, on several levels. Consider MacLean's notion of the Triune Brain in this context and ask, 'What are the needs that might be expressed as archetypes or playtypes, resulting from the periods of our reptilian, limbic, or neocortex evolution?'

Stevens and Price (2000) use Bowlby's (1969) ideas to explain the mechanisms of the development of some mental illnesses in terms of 'attachment', and this can be supported in many circumstances. However, not engaging with the physical and psychic environments in ways that contribute to both the feelings and the realities of meaning, power, creation, exorcism, relationships, abstracts and so on, may also contribute to the psychpathology to which they refer. The 'disassociation' (Wilber 1996, p. 197) from our ancestral contexts resulting from play deprivation, may also be as harmful in contemporary circumstances, as it would not only have the effect of subverting the very fabric of our humanity, but would render us 'dehumanised' (Hughes 1999a, 2001a).

PlayTypes as vehicles for archetypes

In suggesting that play is 'most certainly' a heterogeneous category and that different playtypes may have 'different causal bases, functions, phylogenies and ontogenies' Burghardt (1998, p. 6), demonstrates not only the similarity of the notion of playtypes to that of archetypes, but that one can also sense similarities in their creation in evolutionary time.

It is already suggested above that individual playtypes may have evolved out of profound evolutionary need, and that their purpose may have been to address particular threats to our species survival during evolutionary time. What is being proposed here is that subconscious human responses to these perceived threats may be described as archetypes, and playtypes as their visible manifestation.

Satisfaction

If the satisfaction of archetypal intent is vital to good mental health, and if the manifestation of playtypes is the visible reference point for this, when driven to do so, human beings will manifest an archetypal need to play. If they are able to satisfy this need, then the resultant archetypal play will result in the 'satisfaction of archetypal intent' and the good mental health referred to earlier.

Diagram Three

Archetypal Need → PlayTypes → Archetypal Play
to Play

↑   ↓

Good mental health   ←   Satisfaction of Archetypal Intent

Diagram Three demonstrates how this might happen. The individual experiences a need to have an archetype satisfied. This results in the manifestation and activation of an appropriate playtype. The activation of the playtype results in the satisfaction of the archetypal intent of that particular archetype, and the individual experiences psychic balance as a result.

Frustration

However, what might happen to this model if the environment is unable to accommodate the manifestation of a playtype, or if the individual is unable to manifest a particular playtype?

Diagram Four shows the effect of play deprivation and the subsequent 'frustration of archetypal intent' (Stevens 1982) on a child's archetypal need to play. The sequence runs as follows. The child experiences an archetypal need to play. Unfortunately, s/he is play deprived, or the environment in which s/he has to play is devoid of appropriate stimuli. This results in the formation of a malformed playtype. The malformed playtype is manifested in what Sturrock (2006) calls 'a narrow width' of behaviour, where the playtype is stunted in its display; in chronically stereotyped, repetitive attempts to manifest the 'evolution appropriate' playtype, and in limited ability to vocalise or metacommunicate appropriately. The result is that the child experiences a crisis, brought on by the blocking of the

Diagram Four

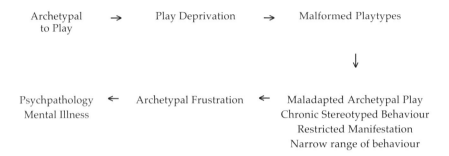

archetypal manifestation, by the child's inability to engage in the necessary playtype.

Imagine, for example, a play deprived child (or a child in a play depriving environment) being archetypally driven to experience ranging, relationships, control, or the abstract, and needing to engage in relevant playtypes as a consequence, i.e. Locomotor, Social/Socio-dramatic, Mastery and Symbolic Play respectively. If the child has the necessary experience and expertise, and if the environment is play enabling, then the child will play in ways that enable the archetype to be rehearsed and psychic balance restored or ensured.

However, if the same child is play deprived and therefore bereft of appropriate experience and expertise, or if the environment is play-disabling and will not support play, then the child will at best only be able to manifest a distorted form of play, which will not enable the archetypal activity to be adequately dispersed and the child's psychic balance will become disturbed or undermined.

It is even likely that if there is archetypal frustration, any acting out of the deprivation the child has experienced will also be archetypal. Thus, if a child when driven to act out an archetype, which is sourced in the reptilian complex, for example, and can only be manifested in Rough and Tumble Play, is unable to do so, then the resultant archetypal frustration may be manifested in typically reptilian – violent, unemotional and dehumanised – behaviour.

This demonstrates the importance for children to have regular access to a comprehensive range of play experiences that make it possible for them to engage in all playtypes.

Conclusion

However difficult the perspectives outlined above may feel to those who interface with children at play, or to those who manage or fund or train, and however deranged it may seem to parents, who simply want to feed, clothe and educate their children and see them attain adulthood as happy and fulfilled individuals, I still feel they should take time to reflect on what is being implied here.

My own view is that there are too many indicators to remain blind to the possibilities I have presented. We cannot ignore the fact that play has been a hugely significant component of our childhood repertoire for many thousands, even hundreds of thousands of years. Why this has been so, we can only guess. Play and playtypes may simply be an evolutionary aberration that we can and should ignore: a prehensile tail, a behavioural appendix with no purpose and little value. Certainly there are many, politicians and others, who would subscribe to that view.

Those of us who have not only experienced but who can also recall the magical joy of playing, who can still experience the evocation of quiet woodland glades; the ecstasy of flying through the air; the singing of wind and water; the thrill and curiosity of sexual naivety; the utter normality of sitting in your own den or cave with the rest of your group; the raw anticipation of ranging and the sheer comfort of a hidden fire; or the belonging coming from group games of skipping and war – we 'know' that play is far more than a irrelevant evolutionary cul de sac, even if we are not altogether clear as to its purpose and history.

In the decade since the publication of the *Playworker's Taxonomy*, developments of great significance in this context have taken place, not least the publication of a number of texts that not only inform us further but which confirm to some extent, this 'knowing'.

Although working with children in play situations exposes the adult individual, the playworker, to many 'firsts', perhaps the most powerful of these is simply the amount of time they actually spend with the children with whom they work. Not just on a daily, or monthly basis, but over years. If they are performing their professional duties properly, they are privileged like no other human beings ever before, to be subsumed into a culture that in the past human adults have only been able to intuit or nostalgically recall.

Playworkers will have seen children regularly engaged in feats of physical, vocal, creative and inventive prowess, which will have left them aghast at their skill, their biological complexity and evolutionary transcendence.

Playworkers will have seen simultaneously the human past, its present and some of its future. This is something they have to ensure continues. Play goes right to our core as humans, to our essence, and without its recognition we will not even take on the mantle of a fallen primate, or an evolutionary also-ran. And this is why exploring playtypes within the context of an evolving neuroludic-evolutionary theory is so important. The relationship between human evolution, brain growth and development, play and the scourge of play deprivation is glaringly obvious to me and a few other individuals, some of whom I have quoted and cited. However, its light does seem to have blinded many others to its presence, and it is imperative that this changes. Play is what makes us what we are and without it WE will cease to be. Over time, without play, we may simply return to the barbarism we came from, or worse still, we may have a brief de-humanised existence. But rest assured, as swiftly as we have appeared we will disappear. And, without play to humanise us, to give us curiosity, aspiration, vision and the capacity to transcend, that is probably a good thing.

Not to realise that this is of such critical importance that it leaves most other considerations in the shade, is a mark of considerable folly. Consider Meeker (1997), who said 'Humanity may have to settle for the distinction of being the first species ever to understand the causes of its own extinction.'

References

Balbernie, R. (2001) 'Circuits and circumstances: the neurobiological consequences of early relationship experiences and how they shape later behaviour'. *Journal of Child Psychotherapy*. Vol. 27, No. 3, 237–55.

Baldwin, J.D. (1982) 'The Nature-Nurture Error Again'. *The Behaviour and Brain Sciences*, 5, 155–6.

Bateson, G. (1955) 'A Theory of Play and Fantasy', in Bruner, J.S., Jolly, A. and Sylva, K. (eds) (1976) *Play: Its Role in Development and Evolution*. New York: Penguin.

Battram, A. (2002) 'The Edge of Recalcitrance'. *PlayEd '02*. Ely: PlayEducation.

Beckoff, M. and Allen, C. (1998) 'Intentional communication and social play: how and why animals negotiate and agree to play', in Bekoff, M. and Byers, J.A. (eds) *Animal Play. Evolutionary, Comparative and Ethological Perspectives*. Cambridge: Cambridge University Press.

Bekoff, M. and Byers, J.A. (eds) (1998) *Animal Play. Evolutionary, Comparative, and Ecological Perspectives*. Cambridge : Cambridge University Press.

Bowlby, J. (1969) *Attachment and Loss, Vol. 1, Attachment*. London: Hogarth Press and the Institute of Psycho-Analysis.

Brown, S.L. (1998) 'Play as an organising principle: clinical evidence and personal observations', in Bekoff, M. and Byers, J.A. (eds) *Animal Play. Evolutionary, Comparative and Ethological Perspectives*.

Cambridge: Cambridge University Press.

Brown, S.L., and Lomax, J. (1969) 'A pilot study of young murderers'. *Hogg Foundation Annual Report* Austin, Texas.

Bruner, J.S. (1972) 'Nature and Uses of Immaturity'. *American Psychologist*, Vol. 27, No. 8.

Bruner, J.S. (1974) 'Child's Play'. *New Scientist*, 62, 126.

Burghardt, G.M. (1998) 'The evolutionary origins of play revisited: lessons from turtles', in Bekoff, M. and Byers, J.A. (eds) *Animal Play. Evolutionary, Comparative, and Ecological Perspectives.* Cambridge: Cambridge University Press.

Burghardt, G.M. (2005) *The Genesis of Animal Play*. Cambridge MA: The MIT Press.

Byers, J.A. (1998) 'Biological effects of locomotor play: getting into shape, or something more specific?', in Bekoff, M. and Byers, J.A. (eds) *Animal Play. Evolutionary, Comparative, and Ecological Perspectives*. Cambridge: Cambridge University Press.

Chugani, H.T. (1996) 'A second chance for Christian'. *The Detroit News*, 9 February.

Chugani, H.T. (1998) *BBC News*, 20 April.

Conway, M. (2001), personal communication.

Conway, M. (2004), personal communication.

Damasio, A.R. (1994) *Desartes' Error*. New York: Quill.

Eibl-Eibesfeldt, I. (1967) 'Concepts of Ethology and their significance in the study of human behaviour', in Stevenson, W.W. and Rheingold, H.L. (eds) *Early Behaviour: Comparative and Developmental Approaches*. New York: Wiley.

Eibl-Eibesfeldt, I. (1970) *Ethology: The Biology of Behaviour*. New York: Holt, Rinehart and Winston.

Else, P. and Sturrock, G. (1998) 'The playground as therapeutic space: Playwork as healing', in *Play in a Changing Society: Research, Design, Application*, the Proceedings of the IPA/USA Triennial National Conference. Longmont CO: IPA.

Fagan, R. (1995) 'Animal play, games of angels, biology and Brian', in Pellegrini, A.D. (ed.) *The Future of Play Theory*. Albany: State University of New York Press.

Goertzel, B. (1993) *The Structure of Intelligence: A New Mathematical Model of Mind*. New York: Springer-Verlag.

Gopnik, A. (1993) 'Psychopsychology'. *Consciousness and Cognition*, 2, 264–80.

Gould, S.J. (1996) *Full House: The Spread of Excellence from Plato to Darwin*. New York: Harmony Books.

Gregory, R.L. (1987) *The Oxford Companion of the Mind*. Oxford: Oxford University Press.

Grof, S. (1975) *Realms of the Human Unconscious*. New York: The Viking Press.

Hall, G.S. (1904) *Adolescence: Its Psychology and its Relations to Physiology, Anthropology, Sociology, Sex, Crime, Religion and Education*. Vol. 1. New York: Appleton.

Hughes, B. (1988) 'Play and the Environment'. *Leisure Manager*, Vol. 6, No. 1.

Hughes, B. (1996a) *A Playworker's Taxonomy of PlayTypes*. London: PLAYLINK.

Hughes, B. (1996b.) *Play Environments: A Question of Quality*. London: PLAYLINK.

Hughes, B. (1999a) 'A Dark and Evil Cul-De-Sac: Has Children's Play in Urban Belfast been Adulterated by the Troubles?' MA Dissertation. Cambridge: Anglia Polytechnic University.

Hughes, B. (1999b) 'Uncensoring Play – Towards an Evolutionary Perspective for Facilitating Recapitulation'. *Proceedings of the 14th IPA World Conference, Lisbon, Portugal*. IPA: Lisbon.

Hughes, B. (2001a) *Evolutionary Playwork and Reflective Analytic Practice*. London: Routledge.

Hughes, B. (2001b) The First Claim – A Framework for Playwork Quality Assessment. Cardiff: PlayWales.

Hughes, B. (2003) *Play and Childcare – Fundamental Challenges*. Bristol: Bristol Day Care Trust.

Hughes, B. (2004) *The Power of Play*. Conference presentation for Sandwell Borough Council.

Hughes, B. (2005) *The Consequences of Play Deprivation*. (Unpublished paper.)

Hughes, B. (2006) *PlayTypes and the Triune Brain*. (Unpublished paper.)

Huttenlocher, P.R. (1990) 'Morphometric Study of Human Cerebral Cortex Development'. *Neuropsychologia*, Vol. 28, No. 6.

Huttenlocher, P.R. (1992) 'Neural Plasticity', in Asbury, A.K., McKhann G.M. and McDonald, W.I. (eds) *Diseases of the Nervous System* 1: 63–71.

Huttenmoser, M. and Degan-Zimmermann, D. (1995) *Lebenstraume fur Kinder*. Zurich: Swiss Science Foundation.

Jung, C.G. (1953–78) *Collected Works*. London: Routledge.

King, F.M. (1984) Unpublished Report.

King, F.M. (1984), personal communication.

Koestler, A. (1967) *The Ghost in the Machine*. London: Hutchinson.

Kotulak, R. (1996) *Inside the Brain*. Kansas City: Andrews and McNeel.

Kroodsma, D.E. (1981) 'Ontogeny of birdsong', in Immelmann, K., Barlow, G.W., Petrinovich, L. and Main, M. (eds) *Behavioural Development. The Bielefeld Interdisciplinary Project*. Cambridge: Cambridge University Press.

Loizos, C. (1967) 'Play behaviour in higher primates: a review', in Morris, D. (ed.) *Primate Ethology*. Chicago: Aldine Press.

Lorenz, K. (1972) 'Psychology and Phylogeny', in *Studies in Animal and Human Behaviour*. Cambridge MA: Harvard University Press.

MacLean, P.D. (1973) *A Triune Concept of Brain and Behaviour*. Toronto: University of Toronto Press.

MacLean, P.D. (1976) 'Sensory and Perceptive Factors in Emotional Functions of the Triune Brain' in Grenell, R.G. and Gabay, S. (eds) *Biological Foundations of Psychiatry*. New York: Raven Press.

MacLean, P.D. (1985) 'Evolution, psychiatry and the triune brain'. *Psychological Medicine*. Vol. 15, 219–221.

Maturana, H. and Varela, F. (1987) *The Tree of Knowledge: The biological roots of Understanding*. Boston: New Science Library, Shambhala.

Meeker, J.W. (1997) *The Comedy of Survival*. New York: Charles Scibners and Sons.

Melville, S.M. (1996), personal communication.

Mitchell, P. (1961) 'Coupling of Phosphorylation to Electron and Hydrogen Transfer by a Chemiosmotic Type of Mechanism'. *Nature*, Vol. 191, 144–8.

Mitchell, R.W. (1990) 'A theory of play', in Beckoff, M. and Jamieson, D. (eds) *Interpretation and Explanation in the Study of Animal Behaviour* (Vol 1: Interpretation, Intentionality, and Communication). Boulder, CO: Westview Press.

Nicholson, S. (1971) 'How Not to Cheat Children: The Theory of Loose Parts'. *Landscape Architecture*, October.

Neumann, E. (1973) *The Origins and History of Consciousness*. Princeton: Princeton University Press.

Ogden, T.H. (2001) 'Re-minding the Body'. *American Journal of Psychotherapy*. Vol. 55, No. 1, 92–104.

Parten, M. (1932) 'Social participation among preschool children'. *Journal of Abnormal and Social Psychology*, 27, 243–69.

Payne, W.L. (1985) 'A study of emotion: developing emotional intelligence; self-integration; relating to fear, pain and desire (theory, structure of reality, problem-solving, contraction/expansion, tuning in/coming out/letting go)', A Doctoral Dissertation, Cincinnati, OH: The Union For Experimenting Colleges and Universities (now The Union Institute).

Reaney, M.J. (1916) *The Psychology of the Organized Game*. Cambridge: Cambridge University Press.

Rosenzweig, M.R., Krech, D., Bennett, E.L., and Diamond, M.C. (1962) 'Effects of Environmental Complexity and Training on Brain Chemistry and Anatomy'. *Journal of Comparative and Physiological Psychology*. Vol. 55, No. 4, 429–37.

Schwartzman, H.B. (1978) *Transformations – The Anthropology of Children's Play*. London: Plenum Press.

Siviy, S.M. (1998) 'Neurobiological substrates of play behaviour', in Bekoff, M. and Byers, J.A. (eds) *Animal Play. Evolutionary, Comparative and Ethological Perspectives*. Cambridge: Cambridge University Press.

Smilanski, S. (1968) *The effects of socio-dramatic play on disadvantaged children*. New York: Wiley.

Stevens, A. (1982) *Archetype: A Natural History of the Self*. London: Routledge, Kegan and Paul.

Stevens, A. and Price, J. (2000) *Evolutionary Psychiatry – A new beginning*. London: Routledge.

Sturrock, G. (2002), personal communication.

Sturrock, G. (2004), peronal communication.

Sturrock, G. (2006), personal communication.

Suomi, S.J. and Harlow, H.F. (1971) 'Monkeys without Play', in *Play*, a *Natural History Magazine Special Supplement*, December.

Sutton-Smith, B. (1997) *The Ambiguity of Play*. Cambridge, MA: Harvard University Press.

Sylva, K. (1977) 'Play and Learning', in Tizard, B. and Harvey, D. (eds), *Biology of Play*. London: Heinemann.

Vandenberg, B. (1978) 'Play and Development from an Ethological Perspective'. *American Psychologist*, 1978, 724–36

van Hooff, J.A.R.A.M. (1972) 'A Comparative approach to the Phylogeny of Laughter and Smiling', in Bruner, J.S., Jolly, A. and Sylva, K. (eds) (1976) *Play: Its Role in Development and Evolution*. New York: Penguin.

Varela, F. (1979) *Principles of Biological Autonomy*. New York: Elsevier Science Publishers.

Wilber, K. (1996) *Up from Eden*. Wheaton IL: Quest Books.

Zuckerman, M. (1969) 'Theoretical Formulations: 1', in Zubek, J.P. (ed.), *Sensory Deprivation: Fifteen Years of Research*. New York: Appleton-Century-Crofts.

Zuckerman, M. (1984) 'Sensation Seeking: A Comparative Approach to a Human Trait'. *The Behavioural and Brain Sciences*, 7.

Index